D0807080

INTRODUCTION

Me? Write a book? Never!

At least that was my attitude. This would be the last thing on my agenda of "things to do."

However, in the summer of 2016, I was at a volleyball tournament, sitting in the lobby talking with a nice lady from another school in between matches.

I was telling her my story and after a while she said, "You need to write a book." I chuckled and said, in so many words, "That is not going to happen."

That would not be the last time I heard that suggestion.

The last person to tell me was a dear friend of mine a little over a year later. All I wanted to do was call him and wish him a happy birthday, but During the conversation, he said there was something he has been wanting to tell me.

"John, this has been on me for a while, but I have been wanting to tell you that you need to write a book. We need to hear what you have to say."

The serious tone in his voice had an impact on me for sure.

With trial and error, overthinking and editing, proofing, and formatting, and writing "off and on" for nearly 2 ½ years, here it is!

I hope this book encourages you, challenges you, makes you think, and makes you laugh!

PS: I formatted this book myself, so if you notice a formatting error, feel free to drop me a message using the contact information in the back of the book. Thank you!

Table of Contents

CHAPTER 1: Dreams of Family

Driving up to an amusement park is exciting for any kid, and that was no different for this eight-year-old. Seeing those large, metal structures moving at high speeds with flashing lights in the distance are memories any kid would cherish. Except, for this kid, my thoughts were probably much different than your typical 8-year-old.

As I stood within those metal structures with the aroma of cotton candy and caramel apples floating through the air, I had a message for my cousin that was probably completely unexpected.

"When I grow up and have kids, I am going to take them to things like this all the time!"

Yes, even at the tender age of eight, visions of taking kids of my own to such places were visualized in my head.

What did not occur to me were some of the issues that could arise with that dream of having a family.

Single Parenthood

Fast forward to November 2004. I am now divorced; not once, but twice. Never in my wildest dream did I imagine that scenario.

By John Helton

I am now also a single parent of three beautiful children, ages 5, 8, and 9. I was already thinning on top, but I certainly did not want to expedite the process!

From experience, most parents know many hours are spent driving to and staying at soccer practices, baseball, basketball, football, gymnastics, etc. of which some I coached. And those were just the extra-curricular activities that did not include grocery shopping, helping the kids with homework, cleaning the house, etc.

Don't get me wrong; I loved every minute of it! Hearing those soccer balls thud against the cleats of my kids as the ball soared into the goal, the aroma of popcorn at the gym as you walked in while hearing the balls bouncing on the court, the marching band cranking up the fight song as your child runs out onto the field, and of course, the roar of the crowd because your kid just did something awesome! No, there is nothing like it!

Then, I got to achieve every man's dream. Weekly, I loaded up those three beautiful children in the family van, Christian metal (yes, I said it) blaring through the speakers at high decibel levels with the hair cut like that of a middle-aged man under a lot of stress, the tailgate rattling to the music, and hauled them to the grocery store. Real men take their kids' grocery shopping!

Completely clueless with the food dilemma, I would gaze into the freezers with the look of someone who just got goosed by a total stranger.

"What do I buy?" "How long do I put this in the oven?" "How hard will it be to get this out of the box?" "Is there more than one step to making this?" Those were all questions that flowed through my mind

2

while I stood in those cold aisles. I was as out of place as a polar bear on an airplane.

With experience and a lot of trial and error, I mastered the art of cooking.

"Get the food out of the box and put it in the oven. The kids won't know any different."

Example:

One of my favorite meals to make was lasagna. Yes, it took a while to prepare what I called home-made lasagna. Think about it: I was smooth in extracting the lasagna from the box, turning on the oven like a pro, and all of this was done at home. That, to me, qualifies it as home-made.

The kids gathered around the dining room table anxiously awaiting to have another taste of dad's gourmet cooking. After blessing the meal and just a few minutes in, I hear this sweet little voice from the opposite side of the table say:

"Daddy! You're the best cooker ever!"

That is correct my friends! I was deemed the best cook in the entire world that night, and that was all that mattered to me!

My Passion for Music

Dad was a singer and drummer. Mom played the piano and accordion.

By John Helton

There were days I would get home from school and when I got to my bedroom, the shiny vinyl of new 45' records would be sitting on my bed waiting for me as a surprise. Every time, I had a genuine excitement like a kid in a, well…. Record store!

Bands such as Journey, Kiss, and Foreigner were some of the music I would sometimes find waiting for me.

In the living room close to the sliding glass balcony doors near the record player stood a stack of LP records, also known as 32's.

Dad would sit in the floor next to the record player with me right by his side. He would share his love for music with me; giving me information on each member, who they used to sing with, what year songs were released, where they were from, etc. I called him, "The walking music encyclopedia."

As we filtered through as many records as possible: The James Gang, Steppenwolf, The Turtles, and ZZ Top to name a few, lyrics of "Just got paid today. Got me a pocket full of change" bounced off our walls.

Even more special, dad would get behind me and wrap his arms around me, grab my hands from behind with me holding a pair of drumsticks, and he would help me play our favorite songs.

On the other hand, mom was a big fan of Engelbert Humperdinck. While she sat at the piano in our living room, I would scoot up next to her to watch her every move.

Hours would pass as we sat on that piano bench together playing duets. Remember "Chop Sticks?" We owned that song!

Other times, I would get on the couch and just listen to the beautiful music she would create.

When we traveled, my sister and I would get a pop quiz from dad. He would drop hints as we both attempted to guess the band playing on the radio.

"Who is this, kids?"

"I don't know, Dad. Can you give us a hint?"

He would reply, "WHO is this?"

Our minds were in complete confusion until he would repeatedly ask in the same tone:

"WHO is this?"

Finally, it clicked. "It's The Who!"

Is there any wonder why I had such a love for music?

Life Without Cell Phones?

In those days, there were no cell phones to distract you, video games were not that popular, social media did not exist, and computers were only for the extremely smart!

When nobody was around, you invented games to play, and…. Wait for it…. created things to do that would be developed as you grew as a person.

One of those creative things for me was to build a drum kit in my bedroom.

I had a large, tall Kentucky Wildcats aluminum garbage can in my room. I took that garbage can, turned it upside down and placed a washrag on the top of it. That was my snare drum.

Gathering several chairs from the kitchen, I would arrange them in a semi-circle in my bedroom and put pillows on them. That doubled as my toms and cymbals. Then, my bed was used as other drums as well.

I envisioned a large arena with screaming fans surrounding me as I placed those records on the record player and cranked it up. I would play for hours and hours and hours. Oh, the thankfulness I have that there were no cell phones or video games in those days. Otherwise, I may have not cultivated a gift I was blessed to have.

As the years passed, I started to desire playing in an actual band. After becoming a Christian in 1990, I joined a band that was highly successful on the local level. We were getting local radio airplay, we were recognized by random people on the street, recorded a record the first year I was a member and won the largest battle of the bands in the region.

The battle of the bands was at the Kentucky State Fairgrounds and took place in this large arena styled building. The stage stood about four feet in the air and stretched about 30 feet across. The drums were perched high up in the air on the riser, allowing me to see the entire crowd out in front of the stage.

The middle of the floor remained vacant much like it did while the other bands played.

STOP YOUR WHINING

We walked on stage, got in our positions, then the MC announced us as a swarm of people congregated right in the middle, filling the vacant areas, and pushed up toward the stage to see our performance. Is this a dream? I was blown away being we were a new band playing in an event nearly an hour away from home and this was the reaction of the crowd.

The music was loud, and all eyes were on us as we ministered through music to the people in attendance.

Three days and 50 bands later, including bands that toured the regional club scene, our band was announced as the winners. That was 1992.

In 1993, I moved to Nashville for a new start in life.

After my first child was born, I decided to give up playing music. Don't most people give up music in "The Music City?"

Being a new dad, I felt it important to focus on my family. But music, too me, was such an important part of my life that it was a difficult thing to consider. I prayed, "God, I want to do the right thing. If you do not want me playing music anymore, then I ask by morning, you take this desire from me."

I woke up the next morning with as much desire to play music as the Rockefellers desired to be broke.

It was time to say good-bye to those beautiful, red drums with the 80's double bass look. A consignment store in Nashville placed them in the front windows for the world to see and that very day, I got a call they were sold.

By John Helton

Eleven Years Later

After 3 ½ years in Nashville, I started to miss "My Old Kentucky Home" and moved back in 1997.

By 2006, the desire to play music again was growing, but not to the extent as before I had kids.

In June of 2006, I ran into an old bandmate at a store and mentioned I would enjoy getting together and having some jam sessions as a hobby. Five weeks later, we were in the recording studio recording a full length, all original CD. Some hobby, huh?

By March of 2007, less than a year after having our first "jam session," we were signing a record deal with a small company located in Texas. That led to playing one of the largest Christian music festivals in the nation, and recording another CD, but much more professional this time.

Walking in the front door of my house, you could look across the living room into the dining room where this metallic set of drums shined with 12 cymbals glistening from the sun beaming in through the back-sliding doors.

The heaviness of the music as we practiced would shake the shelves, turning pictures sideways as we rocked out for the King of Kings.

My biggest fans? My kids.

In our initial CD release party, which would be the first concert we ever played, there was a large turnout in this particular church. After the concert, a celebration dinner was planned in the basement.

As I negotiated the people in the room, a young man and his mother approached me and asked me to sign the CD they had purchased. As my hand clutched that black Sharpie, my 10-year old son reaches up, pats me on the arm while looking at this mother/son duo and says, "That's my daddy." Somebody pinch me.

I was in my element. The fulfillment of having A rocking band that became popular amazingly fast was awesome enough. But I also had three incredible children who were so proud of their dad and loved wearing their band t-shirts to school with "My daddy's the drummer" airbrushed on the back.

Still Something Missing

There was a missing piece to my life. The dreams of being married with kids had a vacancy.

Upon some advice, I was told to write down a list of what I desired in a wife. The list started out:

- A Christian
- Someone who will love my kids as if they were her very own.

Appearance is also important, right? I love the "girly-girl" look with make-up, jewelry, etc. That has always been my style. With that, my hand gripped that pen as the list got longer and longer.

When I approached point #12 or so, I got to thinking, "You are being ridiculous! Do you really think you will find all of this in one single girl?" Honestly, some of the things I wrote down I felt were silly and almost shallow as the mixture of desires in appearance and personality filled the page.

But then this thought came across my mind:

"If God wants the best for me, then why shouldn't I?" Therefore, I kept writing and my list quickly grew to 20.

Online Dating

Having experienced the online dating scene and the issues it brings; I certainly did not want to meet someone online. You never know what is truly behind door number three.

However, with the fact the band was on a record label – albeit a smaller one – I grew a little hesitant about the potential of meeting someone at a show. "Do they like me just because I am a drummer in a successful band?" "Will they still love me when the music is gone?" Those were some of the questions that crossed my mind.

With resistance, I turned back to the computer.

Online dating is like going to a costume party. She is dressed like a princess, beautiful hair, long flowing gown that flows like a waterfall, sparkles in the hair, and a fragrance that would melt any man.

Then, she takes off the mask and you wish you would have selected what was behind door #2!

I noticed a couple of females on a particular site and decided to join so I could contact them.

I emailed them both. Those communications ended as fast as they started. That did not bother me as I was busy being a single dad with my extremely active kids and a band that was nearly a full-time job. With that, I would randomly get online and check for any new potential matches.

There was a feature on this site called, "I'm interested."

"I'm interested" was designed to help you quickly connect with others. That is all fine and dandy, but "I'm interested" only brought up pictures. I know I am a man but come on! Of course, I want an attractive woman, but who is she? Pictures cannot tell you that important piece of information. Women are much more than their looks! Men, did you hear me?

The positive was that clicking on the picture would pull up the profile, so, might as well give it a try, right?

Typically, my age range would be five years younger or older than me, and within a few miles as I did not want anything long distance. That already turned into a disaster once.

I filtered my search, but this time did not select an age range, just the state.

Quickly scrolling through pictures, there was one that got my attention.

"Who is THAT?! "

I paused to get a better look at this picture. Beautiful blonde, curly hair, earrings dangling, well-done makeup, and a stunning smile. This picture deserves a click!

Her profile loaded on my screen as I anxiously waited for the details.

The first thing I noticed was the city in which she resided, but it was further away than I wanted. That soon became a non-issue as I was intrigued with what she had to say.

Reading her profile, I soon learned she loved roller coasters, football, music, and her relationship with Christ was especially important to her.

My mind was racing like a dropped $20 bill in a windstorm.

There was another issue. She was significantly older than me. Ten years and three months to be exact. Quite frankly, I thought that was a typo or designed to throw people off because she looked nowhere near the age listed.

What she said in one particular line exposed the depth she had.

On this site, you can "send a flirt." You simply click on a desired button (Hello, Wink, Kisses, Hugs, etc. were some of the options), and it would send the person a message that said, "John sent you a wink."

Her profile stated, "If you send me a flirt, I will not answer. I am worth more than that."

Wow!

I got as brave as a, well, single dad in a grocery store and sent her a message. My first line?

"Wink!"

This was my comical attempt to let her know I read her profile. It was important to me to separate myself from men who only send messages after looking at a picture.

As I typed out my initial message, it turned into a short story much like it does when I am talking to someone. The worst-case scenario would be getting no response, but I was an expert in that, so I did what I had to do.

The next morning, on Sunday, I decided to attend the early service of a church I had never attended. Upon returning home, the curiosity of whether or not she responded got the best of me. I headed straight to the computer and read, "You have a new message." It was her.

From experience, I knew if the response was short, they were politely saying "no thanks." If it was a longer message, more than likely, they were reciprocating interest.

I dragged the mouse across the mouse pad and placed that mouse cursor right on the message. I clicked on the link and saw exactly what I thought I would: I just wrote a novel and her response was three sentences. Oh well, it was worth a try.

"Hello and thank you for your message. Yes, you are a little younger than what I like, but you made me laugh, so I am giving you another chance. I am running late for church, so I will email you when I get home."

Although that was not what I expected, I was still skeptical because keeping one's word is as rare as finding dinosaur bones in your front yard.

That afternoon, she did as she said she would and sent me an email.

In my dining room sat those drums as I cleaned them for loading as the band was headed to a music festival in Illinois. In the middle of this pile of stands, drum cases, and other drum equipment, I heard a ding on my computer and knew exactly what it was.

I leaped over that drum equipment like an Olympic track star over hurdles to get to that computer and respond to her instant message.

During our discussion, I learned she did not live in the city listed on her profile. That was a decoy as she worked for a family business in our town and was on television commercials. She just did not want psychos tracking her down at work. I am guessing she has the same experiences online that I have!

To add to that, she only lived seven minutes away from me, her parents knew my parents, and the church I went to that day? Hers!

We spoke the next day on the phone. We had similar personalities as we felt like meeting as soon as possible was the best way to handle this crazy world of online dating. However, since the band was leaving to Illinois the next day, I did not have time to meet her before leaving.

Being this is not a romantic novel; I will cut to the chase on this part of the story.

STOP YOUR WHINING

We spontaneously met one day before we had set our original first date. After our second date, she said she thought I was a nice guy, but thought friends would be all there could be. Isn't that what every guy wants to hear? "We can still be friends." Of course, I was not told this until after I fed her.

She really did mean she wanted to be friends, though. The next day, she sent me a "Happy 4th of July" text and wanted to hang out that following weekend.

I was not available on Saturday and when I returned from church on Sunday, she called me, but she sounded upset. I asked, "What's wrong?" "It is Sunday and that is family day. I do not have anybody and am just feeling alone right now."

Because the band had plans to practice that evening, I invited her over to hang out and watch practice. She agreed to do so but had to leave early due to her teaching a singles group at church.

After practice, my kids and I decided to rent a movie. Yes, that is when you had to jump in your rocking family van, drive to a video rental store, then return the videotape before the late fees cost you more than your house payment.

Knowing how being alone felt, I decided to send my new friend a text to ask if she would like to join the kids and me for movie night. As soon as she finished her closing prayer with the singles group, my text came through on her phone and a "Yes" came back almost as fast.

Sherry arrived at the house 30 minutes later and because we had no intentions of dating, I introduced her to my kids.

As we all took our spots on the couch, Sherry sat a couple of spots away from me. My kids then surrounded her like cubs to a Mama Bear. This was quite perplexing as they had just met this woman, but they were so drawn to her. It was almost like she was their mom.

Seven months later in February 2008, we were married.

CHAPTER 2: From the Mirror to the Emergency Room

It is now May 21st, 2008. Sherry and I had now been married for 3 ½ months.

My day got started as it always did, and that was getting yelled at before I even got out of bed. Oh, you thought Sherry yelled at me every morning. No, no, no…. my alarm clock was the culprit, looking at me right in the eyes with those innocent, beady red numbers and acting completely innocent as if I were the reason it yelled at me. So, I did exactly what everybody else does: I slapped it and told it to shut up every nine minutes. it was relentless and after 7-8 snoozes, I just gave up the fight and crawled out of bed. Time for work!

However, this seemingly normal day turned out to be anything but normal.

Gazing into the mirror looking at this pretty face, I had a huge dilemma on my hands.

"How am I going to get those three hairs to lay down like I want?"

A little moose, a little hair spray usually did the trick.

When I turned away from the mirror, dizziness hit me as if I had been spinning in circles in the front yard with my forehead attached to the end of a bat.

To gain my stability, I grabbed the sink with my right hand as my left arm dropped down by my side and dangled, swinging back and forth.

Frantically walking through the house, I attempted to gather my thoughts while, at the same time, trying not to panic. I was feeling dazed while simultaneously trying to gain my composure.

Many of you are probably thinking, "Why didn't you just go wake up Sherry?" That answer is a simple one: Because I am smart.

Truthfully, I could not wake her up because of her sleep patterns. Having fibromyalgia, she would not go to sleep until the early hours in the morning and then would sleep late. The medication she took put her into a deep sleep, so waking her was nearly impossible.

But I did attempt to wake her up once. When I realized that would not work, I decided to try my next option; I called my momma! I told her I needed a ride to work because I surely did not want to drive in this condition.

In the meantime, while waiting for my mom to arrive, I called my doctor to inform them of the situation. They told me to go to the emergency room immediately.

There is now a decision to be made. Although the feeling came back in my arm and it was functioning, it was a frightening situation and now, my doctor is advising me to go to the emergency room.

On the other hand, my son had what they call a "living museum" at school and I did not want to miss it.

As I pondered the situation, I felt it best to do the wise, responsible thing. I went to the living museum first.

The Emergency Room

At the emergency room, questions poured out from the doctor and an attempt to diagnose and solve the situation.

The first examination revealed three possible scenarios. The doctor said, "You have either had a stroke, a pre-stroke, or a warning that a stroke was coming."

Upon hearing this, I had one thing on my mind and I simply had to ask the doctor: "Will I be out in time to see my daughter's soccer game tonight?"

He explained to me they were keeping me overnight for observation, but I would be out by the next day and able to see her game scheduled for the next evening.

The next morning – May 22, 2008 – I was scheduled for an MRI at 6:00 AM.

The Concert in the MRI Machine

I was sporting my fancy hospital gown; you know, the ones where there is always a draft rolling up your backside? I was feeling very macho at this point, so we revved up my transportation, also known as a hospital bed, and rode like the wind down to the MRI room.

19

By John Helton

They rolled me inside the MRI machine for testing, but I was a little surprised at just how confined this machine was. Let's just say I had a 3D view of the top of the MRI machine while I held the little rubber ball that was equivalent to the rubber ball on a bike horn. This was to be squeezed if I needed to escape.

Classic rock played within the machine to keep me relaxed. Being a drummer, my fingers were tapping the rubber ball and table while my feet were moving back and forth to the beat. I was having my very own jam session within the MRI machine. Wait. Could that be the next great band name? "Within the MRI Machine." Ok, I digress….

Thankfully, I knew the songs being I was raised on that music, so playing drums to the correct beat was no problem. The rubber ball in my hand would have been awesome for special effects; however, I had a strange hunch the MRI tech would not appreciate it as much as I would.

"This isn't so bad," I thought. Playing drums to the music kept my mind busy and off the fact I was in some tight quarters.

Toward the end of the MRI testing, sweat began to bead up and seep through my pores. It was starting to feel a little too warm for my liking. The stomach then started to get queasy. It was time to push the button to the escape hatch and take a break.

Naturally, the next thing to happen would be for this MRI tech to roll me out of this tunnel, right? Wrong!

Instead, I hear a voice come through the speakers as if I were sitting on an airplane and listening to the pilot welcome us aboard. The next thing I hear is, "Can you hold on a minute?"

Yeah buddy, no problem. Take your time.

No, I did not say that, but I may have been thinking it! I just simply complied and held on and toughed it out.

Then, finally, the escape from the MRI machine happened. I sat up on the table and waited for my hot rod to pick me up and take me to my room. Unfortunately, I do not remember the trip back upstairs.

Many times, when people dream, they can only recall "bits and pieces" of that dream. You know how it is. You wake up and tell your spouse, "I had a really bizarre dream last night, but I really cannot remember the details. It had something to do with your car parked on top of the house."

For me, that was my reality the next few days, but it was not because I was dreaming.

An excruciating pain in my neck developed to where I could not turn it without the result being a massive throb in my head.

I do not remember much, but I do remember toggling between the two states of consciousness and oblivion; none of which had a sense of reality to them.

The fight for my life had begun.

CHAPTER 3: "I Need My Hurt!"

Just one day removed from going to the emergency room for precautionary reasons, I am suddenly oblivious to reality.

Sherry arrived at my room around 8:30 that morning expecting everything to be normal, but that is not what she found. What she discovered was her husband talking in sentences that were jumbled and extremely confusing.

"Where is my hurt? I want my hurt!" would flow from my mouth. I knew what I wanted to say, but the words forming in my brain were unable to make it to my tongue.

With urgency, she rushed to the nurse's station to question them as to how long I had been like this. The nurses advised her that I was normal when I returned from the MRI testing, but I know that is not accurate. However, she accepted that answer not knowing any different being she just arrived. she then asked what had been done to improve the situation. Their response? nonchalant, "We gave him a Tylenol."

With the excruciating pain in my neck, the pounding headache, and the words out of my mouth not making any sense, the nurse's response deeply infuriated Sherry. It was obvious something was very wrong, but the hospital personnel continued to be rude and ostensibly uncaring.

The doctor on call that day finally came to my room to speak with me. As the doctor asked me questions, Sherry walked in and my demeanor visibly changed. The doctor then turned to her and began to essentially interrogate her.

"WHAT?! Is there stress in your marriage?! Huh?!? He wasn't acting like this until YOU walked in!"

His rudeness and ridiculous implication were quite upsetting to Sherry. Quite frankly, I do not remember how I was acting because I was so disoriented. Maybe that is why my demeanor changed? I mean, I am not a doctor, but that would seem like a plausible explanation, right?

Although shocked at this accusation, she gently responded, "No, there is no stress. We have only been married 3 ½ months."

He then responded with an aggressive and hostile, "I think that is what it is. I think it is stress in your marriage!"

How do you respond to that? How do you convince someone with that type of attitude – especially someone who is responsible for making life and death decisions on your behalf - that this behavior could possibly be a major medical issue and not your bran new marriage?

I do not think this doctor had a psychology degree, but I am guessing he probably watched Dr. Phil the night before.

Following, an E.E.G. was ordered to monitor my brain activity to find answers for my symptoms.

In the meantime, my roommate had family members visiting. They were whispering amongst themselves, "He's crazy. We need to get another room." This conversation continued for a few minutes until Sherry had enough.

She sternly walked straight to them and, somehow keeping her gentle demeanor firmly said, "He is not crazy. He is SICK." They apologized and then offered to pray for me. Do you ever think that if people would simply pray for others instead of talking about them, that it might make a difference? Just food for thought.

The E.E.G. Attempt

It was now time for my test. I vaguely remember arriving in the room where the E.E.G. would be conducted. The medical staff placed me on a table and then started sticking something similar to Playdough to my head and attached some wires. That might be fun when you are five, but not when you are 38!

This is the first instance that I remember the hallucinations I would have throughout the illness. This hallucination had me on the table and elevated approximately 10 feet in the air. Either that or David Copperfield made a guest appearance.

Curious as to the length of this test, I questioned the medical staff and was told it would be approximately an hour. Oh, no sir! No way I am going to be elevated up in the air for an hour with this Playdough attached to my head! I got extremely combative and started ripping off from my head that Play-Dough and made French fries out of it!

Being their attempt to conduct the test was unsuccessful due to my combativeness, they took me back to my room.

Still struggling to get words from my brain to my lips while being highly irritated and annoyed, the only person who could calm me was my dad. He sat on the bed with me as It was obvious to him I was attempting to convey a message, but it simply would not be spoken.

Nausea was now setting in and I needed something to catch what was about to escape my mouth, and unfortunately, it was not words! Somehow, someway, my dad correctly interpreted what I was trying to say, got me a small tub large enough to hold two teaspoons of water, and off I went.

After visiting Helton Falls, Sherry then talked me into going back for another attempt at the E.E.G.

Once again, I got combative and refused to cooperate. I then heard these words from the doctor: "Fine! If he is not going to take the test, then discharge him!" And that is exactly what he tried to do.

My family, knowing the dire situation I was in, was completely enraged at this point. The medical staff overseeing me that day seemed to be the only people who did not think the situation was urgent.

AT this time, my sister-in-law (Sherry's sister) called to get an update. After Sherry explained the situation, she told Sherry to let her get in touch with her husband, "Dr. M," who is one of the most respected heart surgeons in the nation, if not the world. Thankfully, we had that connection. And to think I almost did not date Sherry!

As we waited for instructions from Dr. M, Sherry was attempting to find a resolution in the current situation. She approached the nurse's desk – AKA: Tylenol Central – and asked how she was supposed to handle me in this condition.

"You can drive him to another hospital," they said.

Well, why would I need another hospital if the doctor thought I was OK to be discharged?

Sherry simply responded, "I cannot put him in the car in his condition."

"Then you can hire an ambulance to take him, but you will have to pay for it upfront," they said.

We then heard from Dr. M. "Do not move. Stay put until you hear from me."

He had called the doctor overseeing me. The on-call doctor apparently got confrontational with him as well; that is until he realized who he was talking to. At that point, it is my understanding the doctor had his own change of demeanor!

Dr. M then advised Sherry they had arranged an ambulance to transport me to his hospital about 90 miles away, and he would receive me as his own patient.

Before arriving at the new hospital, Dr. M had assembled a team of some of the top doctors in the area. He and his team were on me immediately; even before Sherry could get upstairs to my room.

Now I am in the hands of doctors who genuinely care about their job and specifically, who care about me.

A lumbar puncture was done immediately due to the amount of pain in my head and neck as well as a plethora of other tests. Boy, those lumbar punctures are fun, aren't they?

However, it did not take long before I started to question the legitimacy of these doctors. Why?

How could they run that many tests including a lumbar puncture; yet, not diagnose me with, "stressful marriage disorder." Nevertheless, despite this, I hung in there hoping they would find an answer that could explain why I was talking so crazy.

Still fading "in and out," Dr. M asked me some general questions such as birthdate, address, etc., while my dad stood by my bedside.

Up until this point, I had worked in my parent's family business for approximately 20 years, meaning my dad was also my boss. With my "boss" at the foot of my bed, the questions Dr. M asked were to get an idea of how cognizant I truly was.

The first question was, "Where do you work?" Still disoriented, I was able to give him our company name correctly. I could not answer many test questions correctly when I was in high school while being in my right mind, so this was awesome.

He then asked, "What do you do there?"

While still fading in and out, I was still smart enough to provide an answer that any boss would be proud of and make their heart happy. So, I answered, "I sleep."

With the negative results from a multitude of tests, Dr. M decided to put me on a wide range of antibiotics to ensure whatever was causing these symptoms was addressed.

But two other test results still had not been received. These two tests were the West Nile Virus and the Herpes Simplex Virus 1 (HSV1).

Approximately 85% of Americans contract the HSV1 virus at some point. Being this is so popular, I was diagnosed with that and sent home. That was a Thursday.

Good to be Home

It was great being home after eight days in the hospital, in my own bed, and relaxing comfortably and ready to get back to life as normal.

Part of my "normal" at that time of year was watching all three of my kids play soccer. That is where I found myself that Friday evening.

When the games concluded, we packed up our chairs, loaded the car, and headed out to eat. What a great evening!

On Saturday morning, that familiar scene was upon me once again. Seeing the soccer fields in the distance as we approached the park, the parking lot packed with vehicles, and the sounds of screaming parents cheering their teams floated through the air.

Unfortunately, on this Saturday morning, I could not make it through the game. Regretfully, I had to pack up my belongings at halftime and head home as the queasiness stirred my stomach.

By Sunday, I was extremely sick and running a fever.

Here We Go Again

As we crossed over into Monday, June 1st, things took a turn at approximately 12:30 AM.

Sitting at the foot of my bed, Sherry noticed something was not quite right. She asked if there was anything she could do. At that moment, my left arm started to tingle again, the left side of my face responded much the same, and it seemed as if my tongue swelled up. I just looked at her and was able to muster out, "911."

As I waited for the ambulance I just repeated(with that swollen tongue sound), "Jesus will take care of me. Jesus will save me." Things began to fade as I thought my time on this planet might be coming to an end. .

I vaguely remember the paramedics arriving. Sherry asked if they could go ahead and take me to Dr. M's hospital, but they said by law, they were not allowed to.

So, back to the original hospital I go where my diagnosis was "Stressful Marriage Disorder."

The gurney was parked in my living room close to the front door.

The paramedics asked, "Do you think you can make it (to the gurney) on your own?"

I told them I could and headed in that direction.

As I approached the gurney, I started to fade into oblivion. I walked right past the gurney as if it were a survey taker in the mall. The paramedics got my attention just before I headed out the front door, which is the last thing I remember for the next four days.

What had happened just 11 days prior was recurring, except this time, it is worse, and my life is now hanging in the balance.

CHAPTER 4: The Throwdown in the Emergency Room

The flashing ambulance lights are now turned off and my return to the emergency room has come.

Those who know me can vouch for the fact I am about as non-confrontational of a person there is. Delirium apparently changes that!

Now back at the emergency room, the medical staff is now ready to perform more tests to get me stabilized. This situation for the medical staff was not going to be an easy one as I was ready to throw down with anybody and everybody around me.

A call to security to try and calm me took the effort of a few and even with my dad in on the effort, they struggled to contain me.

This was understandable as I stand at a towering 5'9, have elite athleticism, and, at that time, toted around a frame of muscle mass weighing in at around 130 pounds. It makes perfect sense it took four people to contain me with a build like that.

A Road Well-traveled

Finally stabilized in the original emergency room, it was back off to Dr. M's hospital 90 miles away. A 4-day stay in ICU fighting for my life ensued.

While in my delirious state of mind, the doctors wanted to hook me up with a catheter. Evidently, the doctors did not get the memo from the previous hospital of who they were dealing with as I was going to have no part of this procedure.

This medical staff was much more intelligent than the prior as they did not call security to hold me down. They called someone they knew, without a shadow of a doubt, I would obey and not cross. They called Sherry.

Along with Sherry, my sister-in-law also joined in to hold me down as they installed the catheter. During the procedure, I looked at Sherry and said in a low-key, slowly stated, and gentle growl, "Sherry, you're making me angry, Sherry." My sister-in-law laughed and said, "Even when he is out of his head, he's still nice!"

Things steadily improved and four days after being admitted, I was released from the ICU.

The Next Step

Because all of the tests came back negative, they took me off-site to get a CT scan for a more in-depth look to learn of any other possibilities.

These test results showed lymph nodes 4 times the regular size, so now, they are thinking it could potentially be cancer. With that, a biopsy was ordered to test the lymph nodes.

It was June 9, 2008 –Sherry's and my 4-month wedding anniversary when I was on the operating table. Dr. M conducted the biopsy that day. How is THAT for having one of your in-laws sticking you with a knife?!

The biopsy was only to be about a 20-30-minute procedure, but took a while longer, causing some concern within the family.

Again – and thank God – that test also came back negative.

But this brought on yet another challenge. What is causing these illnesses? A week and a half into the second hospital visit, there were still no answers. An MRI could not diagnose it; the CT scan could not diagnose it; three lumbar punctures could not diagnose it.

There was one more way to find out what was causing the illnesses, but it would take a miracle and Dr. M explained it to Sherry.

"What we have to do now is find the bug (using the results from the biopsy) that is causing these illnesses, but the chances of that are slim to none because he has so many antibiotics in him, they will mask the bug. If we cannot find the bug, then we must guess at what he has and if we guess, we had BETTER be right, or it could be very, very bad."

So, let me get this straight… My life might be dependent upon Dr. M's best guess?

The Red Sea was parted, manna fell from Heaven, and the doctors found the bug!

Before the discovery of the bug, the doctors knew what diseases I had, but they simply did not know what was causing them. Now, they were able to accurately diagnose the issue and get me properly medicated.

The Diagnosis

During the initial visits to the hospital, Dr. M learned that I was on Humira which was to help me with rheumatoid arthritis. Unfortunately, that Humira completely depleted my immune system from what I was told. With no immune system to fight any disease, I ended up with these illnesses – all at the same time:

Cerebral Histoplasmosis

Histoplasmosis by itself is a type of lung infection caused by breathing in spores of a histoplasma fungus often found in bird or bat droppings. This fungus can travel through the air or be located in the soil. The most common locations for this are the Ohio and Mississippi Valley areas in which I live.

Often, those who encounter this need no treatment providing they have a full and healthy immune system. If the immune system is weakened or compromised, it can be severe and even life-threatening

When it is not treated, it can spread throughout the body and one symptom it can cause is inflammation.

I was diagnosed with "Cerebral Histoplasmosis," which means it traveled to my brain.

Meningitis

Meningitis is an inflammation of fluid and membranes that cover the brain and spinal cord.

In other words, the lining surrounding your brain begins to swell and "squeezes" the brain.

Encephalitis

Simply put: encephalitis is when the brain swells due to an infection.

The two more prominent infections that causes this disease are the Herpes Simplex and West Nile Virus.

Sound familiar? Those are the two test results we had not received when I was sent home initially. With this information, it makes perfect sense as to why they originally diagnosed me as they did.

However, neither were the cause as both of those also came back negative.

Try and picture this:

Histoplasmosis had spread to my brain; a disease that can be life-threatening all on its own.

This caused meningitis and encephalitis both. That means when the lining of my brain was squeezing the brain (meningitis), my brain was swelling at the same time (encephalitis) with NO immune system to fight it.

My friends: That is not a good combination!

There are a variety of issues that could be long-lasting after dealing with just one of these illnesses.

During my stay in the hospital, with the amount of pressure that was on my brain, The doctors told my family, "He may come out of this with the loss of motor skills, brain damage, or end up with the mentality of a 12-year old."

Not only did I survive these illnesses by the grace of God, I miraculously had none of these other issues occur. However, some might argue that me having the mentality of a 12-year old would be considered an upgrade!

This is why my infectious disease doctor, during one of my follow up visits, labeled me as "A Walking Miracle."

Being diabetic, I already was having a bit of an issue with my eyes, and one of the side effects of more severe cases of meningitis alone is blindness.

In the first eight days in the hospital (May 21-28, 2008) I was playing cards and watching television. .

When I was released on June 18, 2008, I was almost completely blind.

CHAPTER 5: Adjusting

A nother challenge now faces Sherry and I as we move forward from the past month. How do I live legally blind? How does Sherry adjust being we are newlyweds? What about working? How do I handle being at my kids sporting events? Then there are the important things like, how do I watch college football? Ok, calm down. That was just a joke; well, at least the "more important things" part of the statement.

These are things I would examine as I ventured through the next several months while recovering at home and learning this new lifestyle.

With the dramatic change in my eyes, we set up another appointment to visit my eye doctor.

"I am sorry. There is nothing we can do for you," he said. You could hear the sadness in his voice as he gave me the news.

With the hopes that something could still be done, he referred me to a retinal specialist.

On this visit, the retinal specialist ran dye behind my eyes intravenously. As the warm dye ran through my veins, the strobe light effect of the camera he used to take pictures flashed brightly in my eyes. This caused my stomach to become very queasy as if I just ate a batch of bad tacos.

Discomfort was the word of the day.

As I sat in that chair with an IV running dye through my veins and my stomach upside down, the doctor's cell phone rang during the procedure.

"Hello?"

Because he answered, I could only assume the call was extremely important.

"Yeah, sure, we can tee off in the morning at that time. Ok, I will see you then" were the words I heard as he concluded his call. Needless to say; I never went back.

What is up with these doctors?

Anyway, the results of that visit came back with the same results: "We are sorry. There is just nothing we can do. Your eyes are as good as they are going to be."

It appeared watching my kids play their sports was now a thing of the past. Instead of watching, someone would have to commentate for me.

What about jumping in the car and driving to different locations? Nope. Not happening.

What about people who walk up to me and say, "Hey John, how are you doing?" "I am great," I would respond. What is the issue with this?

Well, who was it that just greeted me? Sometimes, in a quick greeting like that, there is not enough audio evidence to help me know who the voice belongs to.

Or, what about doing something as simple as heating up ravioli? It is now a bit more complicated.

- Open the cabinet and locate a can the size of a ravioli can.
- Pick up that can and hold it within an inch or two in front of your face.
- Squint as if the sun were directly in the eyes.
- Try to read the large letters.
- Once discovering the appropriate can, at least what you hope is the appropriate can, pull off the top.
- Grab a fork and scoop out the ravioli on what you hope is the plate and not a reflection of the sun on the countertop.
- Place plate in the microwave.
- Locate the adhesive bump on the #5 button to figure out where the other numbers are.
- Set the timer and find the other bump on the "start" button and press.
- Find your way back to the table and get ready for lunch.
- Use your fork gently to locate the ravioli and try not to scoot it off the plate, making a mess. Otherwise, there would be another multi-step process to follow to get it cleaned up.
- Hope that when your fork gets to the mouth, ravioli is on it.
- When you believe you are finished, to ensure none is left, tap your fork all over the plate.

- When no lumps are found on the plate, walk to the trash and dump whatever might be left on the plate and hope you are dumping it in the garbage can.
- Rinse off your (hopefully) cleaned off plate to remove the sauce and hope you got it all.

It is as simple as that!

Help on the Way?

There is an organization called the "Kentucky Department for the Blind" who assists people like me who are new to this low vision thing.

One of their goals is to get people back to work and will assist in any way possible to help in that cause. One way they do this is by providing specialized equipment for the blind and visually impaired to be able to read documents, navigate the computer, etc.

A representative from the organization came to my home and allowed me to test the equipment they offered.

One of the items the representative brought was a large screen, much like a computer screen with a camera lodged on top of it.

The camera would face down to the desk and enlarge whatever was under it such as documents. Those documents would then pop up on the screen where you could change the colors or magnify it so large that only one single letter could fit on the display.

Essentially, it was a very high-tech magnifying glass.

But even with high-level magnification, recognizing what was on the screen was exceedingly difficult.

Then, I heard the line from the representative that I heard from both eye specialists:

"I'm sorry. This just is not going to work for you."

Most all of us know what a painting looks like after it has set in a window where the sun shines through. After a while, the details fade, shapes and figures on the painting are no longer identifiable, colors are faded, intricate details are now missing, contrast is gone, and it becomes very difficult to recognize the image.

That was now my every day, normal vision.

A Second Opinion

A few months later, I decided to go see.... Wait, did I just say, "go see?" Let me rephrase that. I visited another low vision specialist eye doctor.

Before the evaluation, he had his staff take me to more high-tech equipment to see (there is that word again!) if anything could help improve my vision.

We are talking about special glasses, almost like telescopes, but nothing worked.

Then, they tested me on that same magnifying screen I tested at home and the results were the same.

41

It was now time for the eye exam. As he looked into my eyes with his own version of special equipment he said, "Wait a minute. Something just does not look right." I am thinking, "Dude, nothing looks right!" This was not exactly a news flash.

Ok, I did not say that, nor did I think it. It just felt right to type it out at this very moment.

He continued, "When I look into your eyes, I should be able to see the back of them, but I cannot."

With this discovery, he wrote an order for two eye surgeries for my eye doctor back home.

This surgery was not as intense; however, those flashing lights burned in my eyes yet again.

After the surgery, I anxiously awaited as the hours passed to take off the eye patch. Then, that time came.

I removed the eye patch and looked at the television and what did I see? I do believe it was college football!

"Thank you, Lord!" was my immediate response. That was the most I had been able to see for months!

Although still legally blind, and while life still looks like that faded painting in the window, some eyesight was restored, and I can now function in more of a capacity than I was able to before the surgery.

The excitement built up in me as I now could not wait to get back to another sporting event with new eyes. No, not mine. I am talking about binoculars!

I tested the vision at my kid's sporting events and there they were! Was it a struggle? Yes. Did people still have to tell me the scores and do some commentating? Yes. Am I going to complain about it? NO! Instead, I chose to be thankful for the vision I had and did not focus on the vision that had left me.

I can only imagine what people thought who did not know me.

Here comes this man, decked out in the school's apparel, only a few rows back from the playing surface, sporting binoculars. Did I care what they thought? No way!

That includes other situations that I will share in later chapters. It will cause you to laugh or say, "What a goofball!"

Here is a hint: It involves referees!

The Kentucky Department for the Blind Returns

After the surgeries, the Kentucky Department for the Blind returned to the house to present the equipment once again.

That same representative pulled out that same, spaceship looking high-tech magnifier. But this time, when she put a document under it and the image popped up on the screen, I read it immediately! Her reaction was simple:

"Wow."

She then ordered that piece of equipment for me as well as a software program called, "JAWS."

JAWS is a screen reader for computers and reads to me whatever is on the screen. Using different keyboard shortcuts, I can pull up every link on a web page at once, headings, form fields, etc.

It allows me to navigate the computer, tell me which program is at the forefront of my screen, reads the words I type so it is easy to catch those pesky typos, and much more.

I Will Take, "How Much Debt Am I in?" for $1000, Alex

Adjusting to living legally blind was not the only challenge we faced.

Because the family business was a small company, health insurance was not available. That means the near month in the hospital, the two ambulance rides, and all that went along with it were categorized as "self-pay."

Being newlyweds, we already had:

- Two house payments as we were still trying to sell and consolidate our homes.
- Two lawn care bills.
- Credit card bills.
- Vehicle insurance payments.
- Two sets of utility bills for both homes.
- Two home insurance payments.

Let's not forget the three children, all 13 and under, still under our roof.

Now, let's talk about those medical bills (amounts are approximate):

- $140,000 - Hospital Bill
- $30,000 - All Doctor's Bills
- $3,200 - Ambulance Bill

Additionally, a $700 per month medication was needed for the next six months or I could end up back at the hospital.

Never Fear! God is Here!

> *"Bring the whole tithe into the storehouse, that there may be food in my house. Test me in this, says the Lord Almighty, and see if I will not throw open the floodgates of Heaven and pour out so much blessing that there will not be room enough to store it."*

Malachi 3:10

One thing we made sure was to continue tithing to the church. This is the only scripture where God says, "Test me in this!" We were not "testing." We were simply obeying while we stared down all these bills and medical bills of approximately $175,000.

We had some money put away and used some of that for the doctor bills.

Sherry had made calls to those doctor's offices and they were gracious enough to work with us.

One bill was $425. When it came in the mail, it was marked down to $50. Yes, $50!

But what about that medication I had to take that was $700 per month?

At that time, we had a connection to a pharmacist, and he sold us the medication at cost. Even at that, it was still $700 per month! Can you imagine the cost of that medication had we not had that connection?

So, how could we afford the $700 per month in addition to everything else?

During my recovery which lasted for several months, my parents continued to pay me my normal salary. Not only that, they picked up the $700 per month medication.

This was not only possible due to the hearts of my parents, but also due to the blessing of having a successful year in the business; one of our best up until that point.

But there was that looming $140,000 hospital bill.

Still at home recovering, Sherry called me from work and said, "I am going to go ahead and call the hospital to set up a payment plan so we can start taking care of this debt." Being she handled our finances; I was perfectly fine with her making the payment arrangements.

She made the phone call to the hospital and then called me back to give me the update.

"I spoke to them about the bill and told them we were uninsured. When I told them that, they said they would reduce the bill to $73,000 since we have no insurance."

Ok, say what?! Just that fast, another $67,000 in debt is gone?!

She continued, "The lady asked me how much we could pay. While we were having this discussion, I was telling her about us being newlyweds and all the things going on right now. So, I told her we could pay $200 per month until my job ended. She said, 'Well, with what you guys are going through, why don't we just make it $150 per month starting on August 15?' So, I told her that would be fine, and we would take care of it."

Let's do a little math.

$73,000 divided by $150 = 486.67 months, which means it would take a little over 40 years to pay off this debt to the hospital.

Approximately 30 minutes after I was given this information, my phone rang again, and it was Sherry. She was choked up and as her voice quivered, she said, "You are not going to believe this."

I had no idea what was coming next.

Sherry continued, "The lady from the hospital called me back and said, 'After we hung up the phone, I just did not feel right about those payment arrangements. So, I went to my supervisor and explained to her your situation and she agreed. We do not want to be any more of a burden than you are already having to deal with, so we have decided to go ahead and drop your entire hospital bill.'"

Um, what?! Just like that: $140,000 gone in 30 minutes! Now, check out Malachi 3:10 again and tell me if that does not line right up with what happened!

I thought the $140,000 was going to go right out the window over the next 40 years. Technically, it did, but in reverse of how I thought it would. It was poured out of the windows of Heaven to me and only took 30 minutes!

Less than one year later, instead of being bankrupt, we were moving into our new home with only a house payment and van payment. All other bills were paid off!

We never missed one single payment, even with me not working for eight months and Sherry's job ending as well.

In January of 2009, I returned to the family business to start working again. May God receive the glory!

Some might say, "Yeah, but your family helped out and you had connections."

Yeah? Did the family have to help? No. And even if they wanted to, what if the family business was not having the type of year it was? Would I have been continually paid? Even at that, would they be able to pick up the $700 per month expense for medicine being it was a small business? What if I worked somewhere else? Would that employer have helped as much?

What if those doctors did not significantly reduce their bills? How about still having two homes and dealing with all of those expenses?

How many companies have you ever dealt with that, after making payment arrangements to them to pay off your bill, calls back and says, "Ahhh, never mind. You do not owe us anything"?

Exactly!

God places people in your life and He can use them to bless you.

But God does not only financially bless you. He can, well, help you survive three brain diseases at once with no immune system. I would call that a pretty significant blessing!

Unfortunately, some love to "explain away" what God does instead of recognizing the blessings He puts right in front of you.

CHAPTER 6: Laughter Does Good Like a Medicine

So how do you handle such a life-altering condition? I can tell you how: You laugh at it!

Sitting around and whining about the condition does not change the condition. It only makes it worse. Therefore, I choose to have fun with it, encourage people, and try to laugh at myself which – in turn – hopefully makes others laugh as well!

I am hopeful that laughing and having fun with it would cause those in a more normal situation to think about their blessings and for the complainers, hoping it helps them to, well, stop their whining!

Besides, who wants to be around someone who is always whining and complaining anyway?

With that, I am excited to share some "blind stories" and some twisted thoughts that will hopefully make you chuckle!

The American Blind Bowlers Association
National Tournament

When I was a youngster, I was an avid bowler; bowling in three leagues per week.

As the years flew by, my interest became music and playing in bands and bowling fell by the wayside.

After losing my vision, I picked up the hobby of bowling again although I no longer had my own equipment. It was just a fun day out with some guys from church, but nothing remotely as serious as it used to be.

I then taught my son to bowl and that turned into going bowling more frequently.

One Father's Day, he bought me my own equipment. The following Father's Day, both of my daughters pitched in for additional bowling balls. This gave me quite the arsenal of equipment!

It started to become a serious hobby that I thoroughly enjoyed with some competition sprinkled in. Bowling in these "friendly competitions" is how I got the nickname, "The Blind Fury!"

And because I love competition, I got curious if there were any tournaments for those with my condition. Lo and behold, I found the "American Blind Bowling Association."

After researching this organization, I sanctioned through them to bowl in the national tournaments that were held annually.

My first tournament was in Tampa, Florida in May of 2016.

Once the kids and I arrived in Tampa, it was time to check into our hotel. As we walked into the hotel lobby, the kids read a sign to me as you walked through the front door that said:

"Welcome Blind Bowlers!"

Ok, shouldn't that have been an audible welcome instead of a visual welcome?

Oh, the irony!

Follow Me!

This scene takes place, also at the national bowling tournament.

When bowling in the doubles, the team must have at least one totally blind member. My partner is totally blind. We became friends in Tampa and then decided to be doubles partners in future tournaments.

In one of the tournaments, we were all walking toward the door to leave. With all the people in the bowling alley, my partner needed some help. I simply said, "Grab my arm."

He is taking baby steps to make sure he does not run into anything while I am using my guide cane to guide myself and him as well.

Yep, you guessed it:

"The blind leading the blind."

Fast-food and Ticket Numbers

After placing my order at a fast-food restaurant, the girl behind the counter said, "Thank you. Your ticket number is 20-20."

That might be my ticket number, but not my vision!

I Love My Coffee

With the vision I have, high contrast is beneficial for me providing the dominant color is dark.

I sometimes use a dark coffee mug, which allows me to see the creamer when I squirt it in the mug.

After first squirting my typical amount of creamer in the mug, I went to throw away my empty packets of artificial sweetener. When I returned to the mug, I noticed something light colored on the counter surrounding it.

Being the brave soul that I am, I decided to rub my finger across the countertop and when I did, it was quickly discovered whatever it was had a gooey, sticky texture. I will also say, it was delicious! I realized it was the creamer.

But how did that creamer end up on the counter? I knew I did not miss my mug because I watched the creamer as I squirted it. Something is not making sense.

I went ahead and placed my mug full of creamer under the coffee maker and pressed the "start" button.

While waiting for the coffee to fill my mug, I cleaned up the creamer from the countertop.

Once the coffee finished brewing, I picked up my mug and finally realized what the problem was when I could not get the spoon in the mug to stir. The mug was upside down the entire time.

I now have coffee to clean up, too.

By John Helton

A Unique Blend of Cereal for Breakfast

Cereal in the morning for breakfast, at one time, was my favorite breakfast food.

Having a life changing scenario causes you to learn to adapt and do things in ways you never would prior. One example of this is pouring your milk in your cereal bowl.

Here is the technique I would use to do this:

I would first hover my hand over the center of the bowl so I could feel the cereal hit my palm. Once it touched my hand, I knew the cereal was near the top.

When pouring the milk, I would place my index finger inside the "wall" of the bowl to "measure" the depth. That way, when the milk I was pouring touched my fingertip, I knew it would be time to stop.

The same process was repeated on this day and it was a success! Time for cereal!

I grabbed my spoon and took my first bite. I immediately knew something was very wrong because the cereal tasted awful!

My advice to you would be this: Make sure the milk you pour into your cereal bowl is not chocolate milk.

I will have to say, though: while the chocolate milk was bad, it was not as bad as the orange juice when I tried that combination.

Right now, you are wondering to yourself what that would taste like, aren't you?

STOP YOUR WHINING

The Offended Youth Pastor

Our youth pastor had not been at our church that long, so everybody was new to him.

On a Sunday after church, I was eating at another fast-food restaurant. My chair faced the window where cars would pass that had just ordered at the drive thru.

That day, our new youth pastor ordered lunch at that same drive-thru, drove by that very window, saw me in there as he passed, then waved at me.

He got offended because I did not wave back.

I will give you a minute to let that one register.

Thankfully, it did not take long for him to realize why I was not very friendly.

Excuse Me, Pastor

While we are talking about pastors….

My pastor and I, along with some family and friends go bowling at times.

Standing in the pit area, it was my turn to bowl.

As I approached the lane, my pastor started walking as well and ran right into me.

"Hoops, sorry" I said.

His response: "Ain't America great?! You can run into a blind guy and he is the one apologizing!"

Sorry. I was just trying to be nice.

Pizza Delivery

When I was first out of the hospital, we ordered pizza to be delivered.

I heard the delivery driver ring the doorbell and I got excited to answer. So, I made a mad dash to the screen door (the front door was already open).

Unfortunately, when you lose your vision, depth perception is not your friend.

I should have stopped walking sooner.

I do not know if the funniest part of this story is me running straight into the glass door full speed, or the delivery guy quickly taking a step backward and saying, "Oh." I think he was a bit confused as to what he just witnessed.

I'll Show Them!

When I started playing music again in 2009, my band practiced at my house and all the members lived at least an hour away.

Two of the members lived in the same town, so they carpooled to my house. But on this day, they were running late.

I got a phone call and he said, "Hey, we are running behind. We should be there in about 10 minutes."

I sat there with the other members just socializing until they showed up.

Approximately 10 minutes had passed when my doorbell rang.

"Watch this," I said to the members who were there.

I got to the door, opened it quickly and screamed in the direction where I assumed they were, "You're FIRED!" I then violently slammed the door in their faces.

Funny, right?

I opened the door again to let them in and a voice said, "I have a flower delivery for Sherry."

It was the florist. It never occurred to me the next day was Mother's Day. Oops.

The Peculiar Movement of a Drummer

My band was playing an outdoor festival. To reiterate: I am sensitive to light, so playing an outdoor festival is not an easy thing for me.

To get on the stage, I had to go up 3-4 steps. Once getting on the stage, there was a ton of equipment that had to be negotiated: drums, tons of cables, monitors, etc.

As I stood on the back edge of the stage, I grabbed the speaker equipment and held on to keep my balance. I slowly took steps, losing my balance a couple of times, holding onto whatever was available as I stumbled and wobbled in the path to the drums.

We played the show and I repeated the same awkward procedure to get off of the stage.

When I got home, I had an email from one of the stage crew. Remember, this is a Christian band.

He said his mom was at the show and when I was stumbling around on the stage, she turned and asked him:

"Why do they have a drunk drummer?"

The Snow Storm

For this story, I need to remind you that high contrast helps me when the dominant color is dark. But bright colors hurt my eyes and makes it difficult.

We had just received about 15-18 inches of snow and the family – other than me – was headed out that evening.

That means some serious shoveling of the driveway had to be done.

I decided to go out on my own to do what I could. My white van sat near the end of the driveway and that is what I decided to use as a place marker.) As long as I could pick out the van, I would know where I was.

STOP YOUR WHINING

I am shoveling like a mad man with temperatures in the twenties. As I shoveled, my mind was thinking, and pondering things and I got lost in my thoughts. Unfortunately, that is not the only place where I got lost.

I looked up to gauge where I was by finding the van and, well, the van was gone!

The white van blended in the background with the white snow and disappeared. With the sunshine beaming down on the white snow, the glare was – uh hum – blinding me. I could see nothing but white with a couple of dark specs here and there.

To make things worse; I left my cell phone inside. It was like I had wandered into the jungle and the scenery in every direction was the same with no markers to help me escape.

My only option was to scream the name of my oldest who was sitting in the living room. I knew she would hear me because the television was located toward the front of the house. That is where she was when I went outside.

Not the case.

After hearing me scream multiple times, Sherry came running downstairs and said, "Do you not hear your dad?"

My oldest then came out and led me home with her voice.

I had shoveled to the end of the driveway, out in the street, then took a right turn and ended up about 25-30 feet down the road.

Who needs snowplows to clear the streets when you have me?

By John Helton

Driving with the Guide Cane

I was at a fast-food restaurant (seems to be the theme, doesn't it?). As I was eating, I accidentally knocked over my large drink.

A girl from behind the counter came to help clean it up.

Standing next to the table at that time was my son and his friend, Wesley.

"I am so sorry," I told the young lady. "I am legally blind and just didn't see it sitting there."

Wesley, being completely confused asked my son, "Is he really blind?" After my son answered I said, "Yes, I am. I just use my guide cane, stick it out the window of the car to guide me so I can drive."

His response: "Are you serious?!"

No Wesley, I am not serious.

How Will You Do That?

Running the family business, I was typically the main contact when people called in for a quote.

I sat up estimates for my dad to go and look at houses. In a busy time, we might have 1-2 weeks of estimates set up with 2-3 per day at the most. But at this time, we were booking so fast that we had 5-6 per day booked for the following five weeks. It was the busiest time of our history.

When setting up an estimate, I would write the information down on little sheets and slide them in the slots designated for that day. If it was a Tuesday estimate, I would slide it in the second slot, so on and so forth.

Because we had so many, and the following five weeks were so full, it got quite difficult for me to ensure I was not double booking. Having to sort through all of those estimates also took quite a bit of time since I had to use special equipment to read them, phone also placed on the shoulder, and speaking with the customer at the same time.

Normally, I do not tell people while on the phone that I am legally blind. I just go about my business. But because it was taking me so long with this one particular lady, I said this:

"Ma'am, I am so sorry. We have a lot of estimates, so it is taking a while for me to find you a spot. I am also legally blind, and that causes me to go even slower." She sweetly responded, "It is not a problem at all. You take your time."

I finally found a spot for her, gave her the time and date, and then confirmed it with her.

Before we hung up, she said, "Do you mind if I ask you a personal question?" I get that a lot and responded, "Not at all."

"If you are legally blind, how are you going to see the cracks in the wall when you get here?"

By John Helton

Somebody Should Have Told Me

My son played football in college at a small school up in West Virginia.

My parents would often take their 9-passenger van so the entire family could travel together.

On the way back home, we stopped at a pretty nice restaurant to grab dinner.

As we walked in the restaurant that shall remain nameless, I told Sherry I had to use the restroom. She then took me to the restroom door and the rest was up to me.

After taking care of business, we got back to the table and had dinner.

Men know this, but most women might not, so I will explain it.

When a urinal on the wall is out of order, a clear, plastic bag would be placed over it so nobody could use it.

Yeah, I wish someone would have told me the urinal was out of order. I knew something did not sound quite right but could not put a finger on it. And boy, am I glad I didn't!

That's a Terrible Call!

It was during my oldest daughter's middle school basketball tournament.

As stated prior, I would be able to see my kids sometimes through my binoculars when they played.

Because it was a middle school gymnasium, it was smaller. I also have a voice that really carries, so that sometimes can bite me in the rear, but not on this night.

A shot went up and my daughter made a fundamentally perfect box out. For the non-sports fans, "boxing out" is when you put your backside up against the person behind you, warding them off so when the ball comes off the basket, you have position to get the rebound.

Often, the person behind you will jump to get the ball and will get called for a foul due to them having to lean up against the person in front of them.

Here is what happened on this play during my daughter's perfect box-out.

My daughter jumped up and caught the ball on the rebound. The girl behind her also had her hands on the ball while my daughter had it above her head.

My daughter then pulled the ball down and into her stomach area. The girl behind her never released the ball which caused her arms to be wrapped around my daughter's body from behind, almost like a bear hug.

My daughter then bent over, causing the girl to be drooped on her back. This caused them both to fall to the ground. My daughter hit the ground first and the girl fell on top of her.

The whistle blew. It was an obvious foul on our opponent because what my daughter did was textbook.

Instead, the foul was called on my daughter, not the girl who was drooped all over her.

Our fans went ballistic! It was one of the worst calls I had ever seen, no joke!

I decided not to yell and wait for our fans to calm down, which took a while being the call was so bad. Finally, everybody stopped yelling at this official and got quiet.

When the gym got quiet, I reached under my seat and grabbed my red and white guide cane. I held it up high above-the crowd and with this loud, strong voice yelled:

"Hey, ref! You dropped this!"

The crowd erupted in laughter.

Remember, laughter does good like a medicine, so laugh hard and laugh often! I see humor in things a lot do not. (See what I did there? You missed me saying "I see," didn't you?!)

CHAPTER 7: Fast Forward

We are now in the year 2017.

My oldest daughter was at home and in college. My son was away in college playing football at a division II school, and my youngest daughter was nearing high school graduation and preparing to stay home and go to college as well.

Things were progressing as planned.

After Sherry's job ended in 2008, she stayed home and took care of the house and kids while I worked in the family business.

Tuesday - March 28, 2017

Every Tuesday, the kids and I would load up our bowling balls and head to the lanes for what we called, "Tradition Tuesday." Games were discounted on those days, so we made it a fun family outing every week.

Tuesdays were also the days Sherry cleaned the house. She had an interior decorator background with a bit of OCD mixed in.

When the kids and I returned from the bowling alley that evening, Sherry mentioned her shoulder being extremely sore. Cleaning the house likely was not the reason behind it as she was a left-hander, and this was her right shoulder.

She was having some difficulties sleeping in the days following, but again, this was nothing out of the ordinary due to the fibromyalgia.

The symptoms of fibromyalgia are deep pains in the muscles, much like arthritis in the joints. To help her sleep, she took medication called, "Ambien." This is a sleeping pill that would slowly release into her system in order for her to sustain a deeper, longer sleep.

On Friday, we had a nice, relaxing evening.

Saturday - April 1, 2017

With her sleep patterns the way they were, I was typically up first every day. This particular Saturday was no different.

The plan for the day was to do a couples Bible study we had just started the week before. Later that evening was the Final 4, and that was definitely on the agenda as well.

After joining her in the kitchen that morning while making breakfast, we had a slight misunderstanding about something so significant that I am not even sure I remembered what it was an hour later. Most misunderstandings are about that petty, aren't they?

I tend to "shut down" when something upsets me. On that day, I started to react in that same way. But today, I made a change.

Immediately after the misunderstanding, I put on my pouting face and bad attitude and abruptly said, "Just don't worry about it. I don't want anything to eat." I then turned and took my 2-year old attitude and headed toward the stairs to pout privately.

As I was in the midst of my tantrum, and before I got to the steps I thought, "You jerk! Turn yourself around and go give her a hug!"

This, for me, is not an easy thing to do!

I made a U-Turn in the hallway and then a sharp left turn into the kitchen.

With a happy, cheerful tone I said, "Good morning!" I then approached her as she stood near the refrigerator and gave her a hug. The look on her face was one of, "Are you serious?!"

Getting over something like this in a fraction of a second is a gift she possessed and one that I did not. But this time, I was able. She made me breakfast and back upstairs we went.

Later in the morning, she started to feel bad, but nothing significant.

She progressively felt worse in the afternoon, and early evening, decided to take a hot bath in an attempt to ease the pain. This, also, was a common practice when her body would hurt, but it was worse this particular day.

At this time, my youngest daughter was packing to go to Myrtle Beach with my parents. Before she left, I asked her to bring a pain pill for Sherry. Neither of my other two kids were home that weekend as my oldest daughter was house sitting, and my son was away in college.

Sherry would rarely take a pain pill because of the side effects, but this time, she took one due to the intensity of the pain she was experiencing.

As Sherry gingerly got out of the bath while I braced her for stability, she asked for me to rub Bio-Freeze on the shoulder that had been bothering her that week. I took the cap off and ever so slightly started to rub it on her shoulder blade area.

Before finishing the first stroke of application, she nearly collapsed from the pain it caused when it touched her shoulder. It took a quick grasp of the nearby wall to prevent her from collapsing. Her reaction left me dumbfounded. All I knew to do at this point was to get her to the bed so she could relax for the evening.

As the late evening approached and the Final 4 drew near, I decided to watch the games on the main level of the house to be closer to her in case she needed me. Typically, I would watch the games in my "dad cave" which was located in the basement.

Sherry's laugh was one that you could hear from quite a distance. It was no different on this night. As I watched the Final 4, her laugh began to resonate throughout the house. I do not know what she was watching, but it was obviously hilarious!

"Well, she must be feeling better," I thought with a sense of thankfulness and relief!

But when it was time for bed that night, she asked me to turn on the electric blanket. For her to request that was incredibly abnormal.

With her being extremely hot natured, there were times I would have to use the electric blanket in July because she kept the house so cold.

I turned the dial up to its maximum; yet, she was still shivering under the blankets. As for me, I could not get under them because, oddly enough, it was too hot.

These circumstances certainly appeared to be similar to flu symptoms.

Sunday - April 2, 2017

On Sunday morning, with Sherry still feeling under the weather, I contacted our music minister and asked him to have the backup drummer play that morning so I could stay home with her.

That evening, since my oldest was house sitting and could not be at home, she gave me a call to check on Sherry. I told her that her symptoms were that of the flue.

My daughter then told me she had the same symptoms and her (future) mother-in-law gave her some medication that suppressed the flu symptoms. At that point, she went to the store and picked up some of this medication and brought it to the house

Within the hour of taking the medication, Sherry's fever broke, and she perked up quite a bit.

Monday - April 3, 2017

It was Monday morning and time to head to work.

"I am going to go to work for a few hours," I said. "Then I will be back home to take care of you,"

"That sounds good," she said. "That way, I might be able to get some sleep without any distractions."

I prayed with her and out the door I went.

Returning home a few hours later, I found her struggling with some abdominal cramps, but that also was nothing unusual. This was one of the side effects of taking pain pills.

Additionally, her shoulder had increased in pain.

I asked, "Why don't we just go to the doctor?" She resisted the idea, but I still attempted to convince her.

"Please don't make me go," she begged. "I really don't want to lay on those beds."

Over the years, I saw how difficult it was for her to sit in certain seats or sleep in certain beds. With that, I was very empathetic to her situation and eased up in my attempt to talk her into going.

I then sternly said, "OK, but you have 24 hours to get better. If you are not better by tomorrow, we are going to the doctor and there will be no debate. Understand?"

"Yes," she nodded. I then assisted her in getting her back in bed to relax.

But today, she was acting a bit differently. When I would help her get in the bed, she would grab my hand and hold it gently instead of laying down. I would only allow that for a brief moment before I would slowly slide my hand out from hers and make her get in a more relaxed position.

As evening approached, the anticipation to watch the college basketball national championship game grew. Before tip-off, I checked on Sherry to make sure she had everything she needed, then decided to take a shower before the game.

After my shower, I walked into the bedroom and found her rolling around in the bed in agony while clutching her abdominal area. I asked, "Are you ready to go to the doctor now?" In anguish she answered, "Yes."

Because all of the kids were gone, I had to call my oldest daughter again and ask if she could take us to the emergency room. She told me she had to take care of the dogs first, which would not take too long, then she would be right over.

In the meantime, I gathered all of Sherry's medications to show the medical personnel. Believing it was the flu, I assumed we would be in the hospital for a few days, so I gathered all of my medications, too.

Just a few minutes later and rolling around in the bed in excruciating pain, Sherry frantically yelled, "Jesus! Jesus! Jesus!"

With concern I asked, "Do you want me to call an ambulance?"

She responded with a "yes" as if she had just been punched in the stomach. I grabbed my phone and made the call to 911 and awaited their arrival.

The pace in which I was moving across the bedroom picked up while trying to keep a clear head and make sure we had everything we needed for the trip to the hospital.

Approximately Ten minutes elapsed by the time my daughter arrived at the house. She began to assist me in packing but paused when she noticed something wrong.

"Dad? Her lips are blue, and her eyes are rolling back into her head," she said.

My concern grew exponentially. What in the world is going on?

I frantically grabbed my phone to call 911 again as the ambulance still had not arrived.

I raced down the steps toward the front door while trying to make that call. As I jetted out the front door my daughter's fiancé said, "Here they come," as he spotted the ambulance coming around the corner.

I was in the middle of the front yard urgently waving at them to hurry. The driver of the ambulance slowly pulled past the driveway and backed up as if he were hauling a $3,000,000 chandelier. I shouted, "Let's go! Let's go!"

The driver calmly, and slowly exited the ambulance as I shouted, "Let's go! Her lips are blue, and her eyes are rolling into the back of her head!" At my frantic instructions to him, his response was, "Relax, relax."

Let me get this straight: I just told you her lips were blue and her eyes were rolling into the back of her head, and you want me to "relax" while you slowly get out of the ambulance and nonchalantly grab your medical bag?

He took his time, but his partner urgently jumped out of the other side and raced down the sidewalk and into the house.

When the paramedics got to Sherry, they asked her if she was allergic to anything. Because she was able to answer the question so quickly, it made me feel as if the blue lips were only due to dehydration. After all, she had not had much to eat or drink in the last few days.

AS they moved her to the stretcher, she asked my daughter to make sure she was covered up, so her cognitive skills seemed to be intact.

The paramedics strapped Sherry on the gurney and loaded her in the ambulance. They gently pulled out of the driveway and carefully drove through the neighborhood because, this time, they were hauling something much more valuable than a $3,000,000 chandelier.

There was no siren and no flashing lights. Thankfully, there did not seem to be a sense of urgency. That was until the ambulance turned onto the main highway.

Suddenly, the lights and sirens came on while the driver simultaneously gunned it. The situation clearly became urgent.

I had learned that when an ambulance is on an emergency run that if they lose the patient, they will turn off the lights and siren. With that in mind, all I could think was, "Please don't turn off the lights and siren, PLEASE."

There was a sense of relief as we pulled into the hospital emergency area with the lights of the ambulance still flashing.

CHAPTER 8: Life is but a Vapor

In most hospital emergency rooms, the patients waiting to be seen usually sit in a general area. This was not the case for us. Instead, the medical personnel escorted us to a private waiting room.

I was making the attempts to convince myself this was because she was brought in by ambulance and nothing more.

After what seemed like days, the doctor emerged through the door to update us on Sherry's condition.

"When she arrived, she went into cardiac arrest and had to be resuscitated," the doctor said. "We now have her stabilized. We also see spots an infection on her lungs and we are now running tests to learn what that infection is."

I just sat in my chair in silence as he shared the update. It felt like time was standing still.

The theory I later concluded was that the shoulder had an infection in it, too, and that might be where it started as there was a small abrasion on the shoulder blade; the exact area where I rubbed the Bio-Freeze. That was the very shoulder that was bothering her just a few days prior.

Soon after the second update, the nurse came in and said we could go back and visit Sherry in the critical care unit.

Much like the waiting room, all we could do was sit and wait.

Tuesday - APRIL 4, 2017

At approximately 12:30 AM, the critical care doctor approached me to speak with me about Sherry's condition.

He informed me that her organs were shutting down and said, "Right now, we can't even take her up to the ICU because she won't make it." He continued, "We have resuscitated her five times. We cannot continue doing that or it will be worse on her if she makes it. I will be honest with you and let you know that I am not optimistic."

I responded, "Well, I'm a 'Jesus Guy' and believe in miracles. I am not ready to give up yet."

The doctor responded, "I understand. I just wanted you to know." I thanked him and he walked away.

At this point, my sister-in-law gave me the substance of what the doctor was trying to say to me. She is a nurse by trade, so she would know. The critical care doctor, in his own, gentle way, was asking if it was ok to start removing her from the machines that were keeping her alive.

"I don't know if Sherry would want me to do that or not," I said.

But my sister-in-law sternly responded, "Sherry wouldn't want you to let her continue like this."

What do you do at this point? Not only are you sitting there with this news flowing through your mind, but every decision you make directly impacts those who are all around you; people you care about deeply.

My mother-in-law then spoke up and said, "John, we just want you to know that whatever you decide, we support you 100%."

Hearing that gave me a good bit of peace. But still, what do I do? I asked everybody, "Can I go talk to my Pastor first?" "Absolutely," they said.

I slowly made the trek down the hallway as I tried to absorb what was happening.

I walked into the private waiting room where my pastor, our youth pastor, my daughter, and her fiancé were waiting and gave them the update. My voice began to quiver as I explained to them the battle that was raging within.

"I do not want to show a lack of faith that God cannot perform a miracle, and if I tell them to remove the machines, I feel like I am giving up and not showing faith."

My oldest daughter walked up to me, hugged me, and then said, "Dad, you are showing faith right now."

Then my pastor spoke up and gave me some advice that also helped. this coupled with the encouragement from my daughter gave me an enormous amount of peace.

I slowly walked back down that long, lonely hallway to meet with the critical care doctor.

"You do what you think is best," I told him.

"OK," he said. "We will remove her from all but a couple of machines to see how she reacts."

Once the medical personnel cleared the room, I made my way back to Sherry's bedside. I said to her, "Sherry. If you are going to come out of this, this would be a great time to do it."

I heard laughter from my family, but I was also serious because I truly believed she could hear me.

A few minutes later with the sound of machines beeping at low volumes, family members walked up one-by-one to say what they had to say to her.

It was now a waiting game as we sat frozen in time.

Sitting in the chair by her bedside, I felt it important to just hold her hand; something I would not do earlier because I wanted her to rest. Is this why she wanted to just grasp my hand that day? Did she know?

"Thank you for helping me become a better man. Thank you for helping me raise the kids and being awesome to them. Thank you for being you" were words that quietly emerged from my lips.

As the minutes passed, memories flowed.

Life is but a Vapor

The room was quiet and not many words were being spoken as the medical personnel continued to check her vital signs.

As I sat next to her, I felt a hand gently touch my shoulder. It was my sister-in-law.

"John, her pulse just went to zero."

"Ok," I softly said.

I sat there for a little longer just holding her hand and feeling numb, trying to register what just happened.

At 2:22 AM on April 4, 2017, the woman I had been married to for just over nine years entered her new life; a life with no more pain, sorrow, and ultimately, in the very presence of Jesus Himself.

Now what? My mind is now moving at warp speed as I still need to notify my two other children who were traveling home from vacation and college.

Philippians 4:7 states that Jesus is the "peace that passes all understanding." Never has this been more true to me than in this moment.

It is not explainable, but it is real. It is not comprehensible for the human mind to grasp, but I experienced it firsthand.

Several hours had passed and once everybody in our circle had been notified, I made the public announcement on Facebook.

Hundreds of responses filled the page and stories – some of which I had no idea about – were revealed. Stories of her reaching out to minister to people in a way she could only do with the gift she had been given.

Additionally, A friend called me and thanked me for allowing her to minister to him as well. He said she helped him tremendously through some extremely difficult times and her approach to it was like none other.

The Following Days

My head was now on spin cycle.

"What funeral home do I select?"

"What cemetery do I choose?"

"When do I order flowers?"

"Should I sell the house?"

Some of these decisions had to be made quickly so preparations could begin. Yet, I never felt overwhelmed. How does that happen?

The support I received from my immediate family was amazing. Whatever I needed; they were more than willing to do it.

My church family also gathered around me for support with encouragement and scheduling food to be delivered to the house for the following weeks.

Although God's peace stayed with me and gave me supernatural strength, that does not mean there were not struggles.

A couple of hectic days had passed and the day for visitation had arrived.

Sherry's legacy was clearly seen at this time. The three-hour window set aside for non-family members simply was not enough. It was a non-stop flow of people throughout the evening who were lined up out the door.

Finally, after nearly four hours of standing at the foot of where she was, the line of people dwindled down, and it was time to take this aching back home to get some rest.

The Funeral

As the sun rose the next morning, I had to prepare myself for what I anticipated to be a difficult day. At the same time, I knew without a shadow of a doubt God would be walking with me the entire time, and that, He did.

I had been to funerals before, but not one quite like this. It was not a family member of a friend or a distant family member of my own. This was the woman I was married to. This was the woman I just celebrated an anniversary with less than two months prior. This was a woman who stuck with me through a major illness and drastic life change. This was a woman who put her heart and soul into my kids as if they were her own, helping me raise them through some of the most crucial years of their lives.

No, this time, the connection was much different.

By John Helton

Entering the funeral home that day was difficult. As friends and family greeted me as I walked through the doors, my voice began to quiver. My pastor ushered me to a semi-secluded area for me to have some privacy and gain some strength to face the day ahead.

As the service time grew near, the room continued to fill with people. The overflow room was packed and was standing room only. Yes, this was a small example of the lives she touched daily and throughout her life.

I notified my pastor, Pastor Tim, that I would like to speak during the service if possible. If I did not think I would be able to when the time came, I would simply shake my head "no", so he knew to move on.

The service began with wonderful words from him about the woman he pastored over the past several years.

He then read a beautiful letter written by my daughter.

"God's love is extravagant, and there's no telling how far he'll go to prove his love for us. And for us, I think that came in the form of a bonus mom.

Even though we weren't biologically hers, she didn't treat us like we were her step kids. She championed us during the 9 years we had with her, just like her own.

We were her pride and adoration during those times. Not too many blended families get to experience that kind of love, the love she reflected because she communicated God's heart to us.

Her life was a beautiful reflection of our family verse, Colossians 3:23. She gave her all into everything, no matter the pain she would go through because she knew her efforts were Kingdom oriented.

I'll think of her when my sister gets ready for prom and graduation because I know she would be so proud of her.

I'll think of her when we watch my brother play football and imagine her complaining about how hot it is.

I'll think of her when I pick out my wedding dress one day because that was something we dreamed and talked about while watching "say yes to the dress."

I'll think of her when our house stops being as clean as she kept it because she took pride in our neat house.

I'll think of her when I see her favorite things and ponder those memories in my heart.

I'll think of her when I feel the wind caresses my face because I'm sure she told Daddy God to send us kisses for her.

She always wanted a purpose in life and strived to find that purpose, but I hope she knows that her purpose started nine years ago when she walked into our lives.

She greatly contributed to how we turned out as people, raising us by her Kingdom influence, the best way she knew how, even if we couldn't see it at times. And for that, we will be eternally grateful.

Thank you for loving us so well and I sincerely hope we made every minute worth it.

We love you so much, Sherry Berry."

What a beautiful summary of the legacy she carried within our home. But it did not stop there.

When Sherry and I met, I remember her posting on social media under a picture of her and my son, "I finally got my boy!" Yes, she had two daughters, but never had a son, but always wanted one.

Now, it is time for this "son" of hers to get up and speak about the relationship they had formed over the years.

He told stories of her, mainly when he would give her a hard time, which was frequent!

As Sherry would walk through the hallways, he would often grab her with a big bear hug. "Let me go!" she would exclaim." You could always hear her laughing as she struggled to get out of his grip.

During the struggle he would comically say, "But we may never get this moment again."

Please folks, remember that phrase. Yes, when he did that to her, it was all in fun, until he never got that moment again.

The funeral home was filled with boisterous laughter as he told stories of his bonus-mom.

Now, my time to speak had arrived.

Prior to the service, I was a little concerned I might not be able to speak. However, I can only give thanks to God for His amazing amount of strength He passed down to me that day that allowed me to share stories about her.

I stood there in front of hundreds of people with no prepared speech. All I could do was say what was on my heart and mind.

It was only fitting the stories I told would create laughter because of Sherry's quirkiness.

As the service wound down and I said my final words, there was one more special thing I wanted to do for her in my final, earthly farewell.

She was extremely supportive in my musical endeavors, and there was one song on a reunion CD I had recorded just four years earlier that was her favorite. It was entitled, "My God Lives," and that would be the last song to be played at the service.

"My God Lives

And He will never die

The great I Am

Jehovah Jireh

And I will praise His name

Forever and Forever

'Cause My God Lives

And He will never die"

As those lyrics flowed throughout the room, I slowly approached the pink casket decorated in pink roses and placed her favorite flower in her hand; yes, a pink rose.

I kissed my fingertips, gently placed them on her forehead and then turned away from her for the last time.

The funeral was a beautiful celebration of her life in sharing the blessing she was to all of us who knew her.

In the following days, word got to me at how the funeral touched the lives of those who were there.

"That was the best funeral I have ever been to" said one person. Another person said, "I have never laughed so hard at a funeral in my life."

That is exactly the way Sherry would have wanted it with her incredibly unselfish attitude.

She had a laugh that could be heard across a crowded room, a personality as strong as a hurricane wind, a heart bigger than the universe, and a sense of humor that produced jokes of which she was the only one laughing and would say, "I crack myself up" while the rest of us looked at each other like, "That is not even funny."

She was a dedicated mom, "mamaw," daughter, sister, "bonus-mom," friend, and was the epitome of a wife who truly gave everything she had to each.

I witnessed her experience situations that would tear normal people apart. How she handled those situations was absolutely amazing.

She would live between a "rock and a hard place" in order to protect the hearts and feelings of others, doing it without hesitation and with so much grace.

Confidence of a Rich Reward

For those of us who are believers, we have the confidence that Sherry is now living her best life ever; a life that will never end in her eternal home.

> *"My Father's house has many rooms; if that were not so, would I have told you that I am going there to prepare a place for you?"*
>
> *John 14:2*

For that reason, I would not bring her back if I could. If I did, she would slap me upside the head.

Without question, she received her "rich reward."

CHAPTER 9: God Still Speaks

*"So do not fear, for I am with you; do not be
dismayed, for I am your God. I will strengthen
you and help you; I will uphold you with my
righteous right hand."*

Isaiah 41:10

And He is not kidding!

The Empty Chair

I was headed to our Wednesday night Bible study at church just
five days after the funeral.

As I approached the steps leading down to the door, the reality of
the situation set in. Tears began to fill my eyes as I walked through
those doors alone for the first time.

Making it to my seat and not wanting to bring attention to myself,
I did my best to conceal the tears that streamed down my cheeks.

Just two weeks prior, the seat next to me was filled as Sherry sat
next to me as she always did.

But on this night, it was empty.

The Vision

One of our other ministers taught that night. He concluded in a way that was not typical of a Wednesday night service. He asked us to stand and worship while a CD of worship music played over the speakers.

Within a few seconds, there was a gentle tap on my right shoulder. It was a young man from our church who wanted to speak to me.

"John, I have a testimony for you." I thought the timing was a bit odd being we just entered worship. I quietly responded with, "OK" having no idea what I was about to hear.

"I was at a youth conference last weekend and while I was in deep worship, I saw Sherry dancing with Jesus."

In an instant, immediately after hearing this, I saw a vision that lasted maybe a quarter of a second.

Sherry was standing in an open field. To the right of her in this vision was a vague figure.

I noticed her curly, blonde hair but this time, it had an extremely beautiful glow to it. But I could not see her face.

The most prominent characteristic of this vision was the peach-colored dress she was wearing.

Where did this come from? That is a lot of details to think up in such a short moment.

I looked at this young man who was celebrating his 18th birthday on this day and gently said, "Thank you." I turned around to my seat and the flood gates of tears opened. I wept at my seat for 5-10 minutes.

With the way my mind works and the way I overthink, I was still contemplating what I just saw.

"Was that me that thought that, or did God just show me Sherry in Heaven?"

I was not convinced it was just me, nor was I convinced it was from God, either. I just did not know, but how am I supposed to find out?

Three Days in a Row

We are now a little over two weeks after Sherry's passing.

Like most people, I have a routine when I get up and get my day started.

Because I have incredibly awesome parents, they told me to pack my things from my office and move into my house to make things easier. And that, I did!

My office was now in my home and things became much more simplified. I was now running the business without having to leave the house.

When you are legally blind and suddenly having to take care of everything, this is a welcomed change.

My Routine

In the living room on the main level of the house, I had what I called "The Prayer Chair."

I would get up in the mornings and do a little exercising – and I do mean a little! After that, I would fix my creamer with some coffee in it and head to my prayer chair with my electric razor in hand.

In the prayer chair, I would shave this pretty face and beautiful bald head (leave me alone and let me dream) and spend that time talking to my Heavenly Father.

When I was finished shaving, I would head upstairs to my computer and read God's Word.

This was my daily, morning routine just about every single day.

To reiterate from an earlier chapter:

On my computer, I have a screen reader program called, "JAWS." This program is for the visually impaired and blind to help them navigate the computer and reads to them what is on the screen. That is how I read and send emails, read documents, and read web pages.

Additionally, next to my desk, I have another piece of special equipment called a "CCTV." This has a screen, much like a computer.

Under the elevated screen is a tray to place documents. A camera above the tray captures the documents and displays them on the screen.

I can enlarge or reduce the documents to read them, invert colors, change the color scheme, and even have the CCTV scan the document and read it to me if desired. That gives me the choice to read the text myself or have it read to me.

Wednesday – Day 1

After my prayer time on this particular Wednesday, I thought it would be cool to read out of the Bible Sherry used instead of reading on my computer. This was possible for me using the CCTV.

I went upstairs, planted my caboose in my chair, grabbed the Bible, opened it up and put it under the camera to magnify the text on the screen. During this process, I strongly felt like God had a specific word for me.

I randomly opened the pages and began to read. As my eyes scrolled the magnified text, I did not feel that was where I was supposed to be reading. But "in my spirit" as they would say, I knew there was a specific word waiting. So, how do I find it? Where am I supposed to be reading this word/scripture I believed was for me?

It is interesting, when we are not sure of what to do, God has a way of leading us if we listen!

I then noticed a bump in the pages further back and decided to turn there. What I discovered in those pages – that bump – was a foam crown given to her at a Wednesday night Bible study. I recognized the shape of the crown using the CCTV. Written across the crown, in Sherry's handwriting, was the word, "Heaven."

The passage there was exactly where I was supposed to be; the very word God had for me that day. As I read it, I knew without a shadow of a doubt that was it.

> *"Therefore my brothers and sisters, make every effort to confirm your calling and election. For if you do these things, you will never stumble, and you will receive a rich welcome into the eternal kingdom into our Lord and Savior Jesus Christ."*
>
> *2 Peter 1:10-11*

There it was!

Was it simply irony the verse God had for me happened to be marked by a crown with the word "Heaven" on it, and the passage happened to talk about receiving a rich welcome into God's eternal Kingdom?

No! God sent me to this very verse to comfort me; letting me know Sherry was now in this glorious Kingdom and received a "rich welcome!"

Doesn't that sound familiar to the vision I saw that Wednesday night at church?

Thursday – Day 2

The next day, I was back in the prayer chair with my cup of creamer with a touch of coffee and my electric razor.

With the buzzing of the electric razor sounding like bees circling my head, I was giving thanks to God for helping me in this time. The words from my mouth that day were, "Thank you, God for helping me survive another day."

My heart behind this prayer was not one of defeat or complaining. I was truly thankful that He had given me so much strength during this difficult time.

Once those words were spoken, it was like He reached down and placed His hand over my mouth to get me to hush, which proves God can still do miracles.

In His gentle voice, He responded with these encouraging words:

"I did not create you to be a 'survivor,' I created you to be a 'conqueror'!"

These words were so comforting and encouraging!

They can be found here:

> *"No, in all these things we are more than*
> *conquerors through Him who loves us."*
>
> *Romans 8:37*

Often times, we know what the Word of God says, and we encourage others with it. But when it comes to believing the Word about ourselves, it is sometimes difficult to accept.

His still, small voice comforted me that day and told me exactly what I have been created to be.

We need to believe the Word of God and what it says we are!

Friday – Day 3

Guess where I am this morning? Yes, the prayer chair!

As I concluded my prayer time and got up, I heard, "Go to the book of John."

"John?" I thought. It kind of dazed me for a moment when I heard this, but to the book of John I go!

I picked up the Bible and prepared to place it under the CCTV for more reading. But this time, something was different.

Before I could place it on the tray under the camera, I noticed something hanging out of the pages I had never seen or felt. It was a ribbon which ended up being a bookmark.

As anybody would do, I grasped that ribbon, slowly slid it up and opened the Bible to the pages the ribbon marked. Would you like to take a wild guess as to which book was marked? You got it. It was the book of John!

Are you kidding me?!

Because it took me directly to the book of John, I knew what I was about to read was specifically for me. Isn't that cool?

I magnified the text and adjusted the tray to learn what God was about to speak. The passage I landed on was this:

> *"Afterward Jesus appeared again to His*
> *disciples, by the sea of Galilee.*

It happened this way: Simon Peter, Thomas also known as Didymus), Nathanael, from Canain Galilee, the sons of Zebedee, and two other disciples were together.

"I'm going out to fish," Simon Peter told them, and they said, "We'll go with you." So they went out and got into the boat, but that night they caught nothing.

Early in the morning, Jesus stood on the shore, but the disciples did not realize it was Jesus.

He called out to them, "Friends, haven't you any fish?" No," they answered.

He said, "Throw your nets on the right side of the boat and you will find some." When they did, they were unable to haul the net in because of the large number of fish."

John 21:1-6

I headed back downstairs for another cup of coffee as I pondered why God would send me to this specific scripture.

The conclusion I came to as I meditated on this was, "Yes, Sherry was absolutely a fisher of men." She loved counseling people and helping them through difficult times; using the gift God gave her.

About halfway down the steps, God stopped me in my tracks yet again and said, "No! That was not about Sherry. That was for you! You are not finished yet!"

Wouldn't it be awesome if there was a camera set up to catch my facial expressions during these moments?

I was blown away. He is truly an amazing God!

> *"The Lord is close to the broken-hearted and saves those who are crushed in spirit."*
>
> *Psalm 34:18*

The Peach-Colored Dress

Remember the story of the peach-colored dress? I hope so since it was at the beginning of this chapter!

Approximately three months after I saw that vision that I could not determine whether it was God or me, I was in our church foyer speaking with a lady named Shirley.

Shirley leads a ministry called "Living Free," in which Sherry was a facilitator. We were talking about doing something in Sherry's memory for that ministry.

We then began talking about Sherry and how well she is doing.

I said, "I can't help but to be happy for her. As much as she struggled physically, knowing she is now in no more pain and dancing makes me happy."

Shirley's response stunned me.

"Yeah, she is up there dancing in her peach-colored dress!"

I was absolutely rocked to the core.

"What did you just say?!"

Shirley was a bit perplexed at my response. She answered me as if she were asking a question, "She is dancing in her peach-colored dress?"

"Shirley," I said, "Why did you say peach-colored dress?"

It was as if I was giving her a pop quiz she was not prepared to take.

Again, with the tone of asking a question she responded, "Because she liked coral colors?"

"Right, Shirley" I added, "But why did you say peach? Did you ever see her in a peach dress?"

"No, I didn't," she answered.

At that point, I began explaining the vision I had 2-3 months prior on that particular Wednesday night. Shirley was in as much shock as I was, but this was no doubt a confirmation!

I finally had my answer.

God showed me a vision of Sherry in Heaven and there is no doubt the vague figure next to her was Jesus Himself.

But it did not stop there.

Again?

A couple of weeks after that, my son and I were leaving the bowling alley when my phone rang. It was Sherry's daughter.

Sherry and her granddaughter used to play "makeup" and she would dress in Sherry's high heels.

Sherry's granddaughter said she could not remember what "mamaw" looked like, so she was told to close her eyes and think of her.

When asked what she saw she said, "I see mamaw. She is in an orangy colored dress."

Not high heels, nothing about earrings, but all about that dress!

At this time, Sherry's granddaughter was eight.

His Love is Deep!

"Who are we, that you are mindful of us, Lord?"
(My version!)

Psalm 8:4

These stories are just a small example of the depth and love that God has for His people. I must be pretty special to Him for Him to think enough of me to comfort me in these ways.

The great thing is that He loves you every bit as much as He does me! What He does for me, He will do for you!

CHAPTER 10: Stop Your Whining!

How you respond to difficult circumstances is key to moving forward, and that goes for many different aspects of life.

I did not plan on bowling in the 2017 American Blind Bowling Association (ABBA) national tournament. But when Sherry passed away, I started to think about it a little more. After discussing it with my parents, we felt it would be good for me to go, and that is what I did.

The ABBA National Tournament

Toward the end of May, we (two of my kids and I) boarded a plane and headed to Phoenix, AZ for me to compete.

The doubles and singles tournaments are held on the same night, back-to-back with the double's tournament first.

In the double's tournament, it was as if I had never bowled before. The struggle was real. My scores were embarrassing, and it appeared it was going to be a long night. But moping and whining would not have changed the circumstances (or my scores!).

After the double's tournament, we had a 10-15 minute break before the start of the singles tournament.

So, I tried to get my head screwed on straight, let go of my frustrations, and focus on the tournament ahead.

My first two scores in the singles were not bad, but I knew I had to step it up a notch if I wanted to have a chance to win this thing. I felt the first two games had me in the running, but another score like the first two would not cut it.

In the last game, it felt like I was bowling pretty well, but I did not want to know my score until the last ball was thrown to keep the pressure off of me.

I finished my game and the score finally flashed on the screen, but I obviously could not see it.

I was a bit hesitant to learn what I just bowled because, too often, I feel like I bowl well and then someone tells me my score. Many times, it is much lower than what I expected. I usually respond with a disappointed, "Are you kidding me?"

So, with a bit of cautious optimism, feeling like I bowled a rather good score, I asked my son, "What did I shoot?"

"226," he said.

At that point, with that score, I knew there was at least a chance.

When the results finally came in, it was an enormous blessing when I realized I was the scratch singles national champion.

There was also a little bonus in that tournament:

There is a sighted division, and the scratch singles national champion? My son!

God tremendously blessed me with that honor. But what if I decided to stay home and mope, whine, complain, and feel sorry for myself?

And even though I went, what if I did not have a "mindset change" in the middle of the two tournaments? It is simple:

Same mindset equals same results!

The scores I bowled in the doubles tournament likely would have carried over to the singles if I marinated in my pity and disappointment. Had that been my mindset, I pretty much guarantee no title would have happened and I would have completely missed it.

So, **STOP YOUR WHINING** so you do not miss what God still has for you! Whining can cause you to miss the most beautiful of blessings

Called to the Speaking Ministry

In June 2009, with my new band, I was about to do my first concert ever as a legally blind drummer at a small, city park.

I do not want to go into details why I was annoyed at this situation, but what I will say is that while in transit to the show, I did not have a particularly good attitude. I felt like I should have been playing a show in another location much bigger than where I was headed.

As soon as I started to grumble and whine in my thoughts, I stopped and said, "God, I am sorry. If you wanted me to be playing at (the other show), then that is where I would be. If you have someone up here that I am supposed to reach, then let's do it!"

We were the first band to play that day.

We finished our set and as my band members were moving their equipment off stage, the next band was moving theirs on it. But for me, I used the stage drums; therefore, I had no personal equipment to move.

While the guys were moving equipment, the concert promoter walked up and asked, "Would you like to give about a 10-minute testimony while they get set up?"

I was surprised, but eager to share, so I agreed to give whatever message God put on my heart. It is not difficult to get me to talk, and that is especially true when it comes to the things of God.

So, I did my thing and that was it. Or was it?

A little later, I was standing with a group of people just hanging out. A young lady walked up to me and said, "John, my dad wanted me to come and tell you 'thank you.' He said he really needed to hear what you had to say."

Whoa! That was unexpected! I was so blown away and humbled!

We then headed to our guitarists house to watch the video of the show. As I sat on the couch, a girl walked to the coffee table in front of me, leaned over and said, "John, thank you for what you said today. I needed that."

I was absolutely astonished. It did not take me long to realize I was not there to "just" play music. God, in my imperfections, had another purpose for me.

The next evening at home, the feeling of that day still lingered. When God uses me, it is so humbling, and extremely fulfilling.

I was expressing my heart with Sherry about this and, while doing so, the thought came to me, "I wonder if God is calling me to the speaking ministry?" As I pondered this thought, Sherry said, "Do you think God is calling you to the speaking ministry?"

Well, I do now!

I responded to her with an excited, "I was just thinking that same exact thing!"

And that is when the speaking ministry began.

This is just another example of God blessing me. Would He have done that if I complained without changing my mindset? I cannot answer that question. But what I will say is this:

God has a much more difficult time hearing your prayers when your whining is louder!

You may not be in a situation or circumstance that you would prefer, but it very well might be exactly where God wants you. That is what happened to me that day.

So, instead of complaining like I started to do that day, be thankful that He will use you if you allow Him, irrespective of your situations!

"And we know that in all things God works for the good of those who love Him, who are called according to His purpose."

Romans 8:28

Whether you believe it or not, whatever your status or condition, you have a purpose if you are breathing. My hunch is, that if you are reading this right now, you are doing just that. That tells me that no matter who you are, there is a purpose for your life.

"For we are God's handiwork, created in Christ Jesus to do good works, which God prepared in advance for us to do."

Ephesians 2:10

See? I told you!

While bowling bad in a tournament or playing a city park is nothing compared to losing a spouse or vision, the response to those situations is still important.

Yes, there is a time for mourning and a time for tears, both of which I certainly experienced, but somehow, someway, you have to put your feet to the ground and refuse to let situations defeat you.

I believe the strength in doing this can be summed up with this:

Rock vs. Sand

"Therefore everyone who hears these words of mine and puts them into practice is like a wise man who built his house on the rock.

The rain came down, the streams rose, and the wind blew and beat against that house, yet it did not fall, because it had its foundation on the rock.

But everyone who hears these words of mine and does not put them into practice is like a foolish man who built his house on sand. The rain came down, the winds blew and beat against that house, and it fell with a great crash."

Matthew 7:24-27

This is Jesus talking. He is using a simile here where you are the house and He is the rock. How you come through the storms of life is determined on where you build your foundation.

Without Christ, I cannot imagine how difficult these situations would have been. I am pretty certain a "great crash" would have ensued.

Where is your foundation built?

Another key component is how you live your life right now.

Regarding Sherry, my marriage with her was without regret.

When there were issues, we would always, and I mean ALWAYS, discuss them in a calm tone and come to a resolution. There were times where I could feel my emotions start to get a little fired up and somehow, she stayed calm, cool, and collected. In turn, that helped me do the same.

> *"A gentle answer turns away wrath, but a harsh word stirs up anger."*

Proverbs 15:1

Remember the story of the misunderstanding in the kitchen? What if that misunderstanding turned into an argument, ruining the weekend, or at least some of it? Remember, I tend to "shut down" when I am upset. But on that weekend, I did not do that. Thankfully, that was the case because I had no idea that three days later, I would be planning her funeral.

One of the last moments I had with her, excluding the time she was not feeling well, was that hug. Had I not hugged her, what I am writing right now would be much different. It would be laced with regret, without question.

Why take a chance? Why risk throwing away a moment you will never get back?

Husband and Wife

The relationship between a husband and wife is a special one. It is the very relationship God deems as more important than any other relationship on the face of the planet; yet, we do not treat it that way and that is truly a shame.

"Marriage is to be held above all, and the marriage bed undefiled."

Hebrews 13:4

Anything we do that negatively impacts our spouse can be defined as "defiling the marriage bed." It is not just sexual immorality.

We complain about our spouse, nit-pick over everything, always find the negative about them instead of cherishing the "little things," spend more time with everything and everybody else rather than them, then cannot figure out why our marriage is so difficult and unfulfilling!

My friends, please listen to me; Do not wait until the funeral home to cherish your spouse!

If you are not doing this already, reflect back to when you dated and start chasing your spouse like you did then. I promise; it is worth your time and effort! You do not want to be in my position and "wish" you would have spent more time valuing them. The time is now!

Every minute that passes by is gone forever. What did you do with that minute? How will you remember it? Whether you are productive with it or you waste it, that moment is gone. So, cherish life and take advantage of the blessings God has put right in front of you.

Being Legally Blind

When I lost a lot of vision, I had two choices:

- I could mope, complain, gripe, and be miserable.
- I could stay positive and have a blast!

Which one of those two sounds like the best option to you? If you picked number two, then why do you revert to number one in some of your situations?

I could wake up every morning and act like a 3-year old, throw myself on the ground and kick my feet while saying, "I hate this! I cannot see, cannot drive, have to use all of this special equipment to function, while everybody else gets to get up, go to work, and see perfectly! Woe is me; woe is me; woe is me!"

And when I get up from that temper tantrum, I would still be legally blind, but much more miserable!

Not only that, but I would make the people around me miserable, too!

Or I could wake up every day and easily find the blessings God has placed all around me.

Which person do you want to be around?

The negative can be found in anything. Likewise, so can the positive. It is all in your mindset. You get to make the choice!

I will put it to you as simple as I can:

Being blind is horrible if you make it that way. But being blind is a blast… if you make it that way!

Would I take my vision back? Absolutely! I believe God will restore my vision (Isaiah 53:5) but until then, I want to challenge people, encourage people, and make them laugh!

Is it frustrating sometimes? Of course! But dwelling on it is not an option.

> *"Open my eyes that I may see wonderful things in your law."*
>
> *Psalm 119:18*

Many have 20/20 vision; yet, they are still blind. Is that you?

Perspective

I saw a Facebook post…. Ok, I did not "see" it, but I read it…. leave me alone. You knew what I meant!

Anyway, this post said, "Just closed on my house today and now I am stuck in the line at Walmart. Ugh."

I responded, "Did you drive to Walmart?" The response was, "Ok, John… I hear you."

Perspective!

While running the family business, I met a lot of people and became friends with several of them.

One particular gentleman became a favorite because he could dish it out just as well as I could.

One day he called me and when I asked how he was doing he said, "Well, not too well." I asked him why and he said, "I knew I should not have cracked on you about your vision."

I responded, "Why, what is wrong?"

"Well man, about a year ago, I went to my optometrist because I noticed my vision getting worse. We just assumed it was a change in my vision. He got me some glasses and my vision was better for a while.

Several months later, I noticed my vision getting worse, so I went back. Dude, I am going to have to have cataract surgery on both of my eyes. Not only that, it is going to cost me $5,000 to have it done."

The tone of his voice was one of much sadness. So, I decided to do what I do.

"Are you really calling a blind guy to complain that you have to have surgery to get your vision back? And you have the $5,000 to have it done? Do you know how much money I would give to get my vision back, and you are complaining to me?!"

My tone was serious but with a comedic delivery.

One of the last things he said to me before we hung up was, "Man, I am so glad I called you. I have tears running down my cheeks from laughing so hard!"

Perspective!

Every morning when you wake up, the first thing that crosses your mind or comes out of your mouth should be, "Thank you, Lord, for my blessings!"

An Attitude of Gratitude

It is 6:00 AM on a cold, winter Monday morning when your alarm goes off. The exhausting weekend of kid's sports and travel causes you to hit the snooze button at least three times before crawling out of bed.

Your three kids – all in elementary or junior high school – are running around the house a bit hyper because they just ate their sugar-laced pop-tarts

You now go outside to start your 20-year old car covered in ice and snow from the overnight winter weather. You grab the slider and shove it to the right where the red dots are to maximize the heat. Forcing the knob to the defrost setting and knowing it will take at least 20 minutes for this old thing to clear the windows, you pray there is enough gas in the tank to heat the car and get to the gas station to fill it up on your way to work.

You then quickly run back into your warm abode to slam down your breakfast your wife made, although the pancakes are not quite as good as your favorite restaurants.

Scarfing down your pancakes, your mind is dreading the day ahead with the meetings you have to lead with your staff.

"I cannot wait until 5:00 gets here" are the thoughts that go through your mind.

You finally arrive home at 5:30 PM after a long day at work. You walk in the door where your wife is waiting and says, "I'm sorry, honey. I was not able to get dinner ready. A friend called and needed some advice, so we were on the phone for a few hours. I still had to get laundry done from over the weekend and time just got away."

Frustrated, you start mumbling under your breath, head to the pantry and fix yourself a man's meal; the dinner of a champion: cereal!

Pushing through that, the kids now need a little help with their homework. After a couple of hours, you take a hot shower and get ready to chill out for the evening. You and your wife sit on the couch and watch your favorite show, then crawl into bed and talk about your day.

Pretty stressful and draining day, huh? It is? Are you sure?

Let us take a moment to review:

- You woke up and got out of bed on your own when someone else is confined to a wheelchair.
- You woke up in your dwelling place while others are living in a cardboard box downtown.
- You have hot water while others are taking baths in street puddles.
- You have healthy kids while a barren mother dreams of having one single child.
- You had money to travel this past weekend while some do not have money to eat.

- You have money to fill up your gas tank while some walk to their destination... and sometimes, in the rain.
- Your car runs while others hope their bicycle chain does not break.
- You have a decent paying job while the guy around the corner works three jobs just to put food on the table for his family and cannot make it to a majority of his kid's sporting events.
- You have a caring wife while your friend across town has one that cares nothing about him.
- You have something to eat while others would beg for a bowl of cereal or even a couple of crackers.
- The cable bill is paid so that you can watch your favorite show with your wife while others are alone.
- Your wife wants to converse with you before going to bed while many are having marriage struggles.

So, what is the problem again? In other words,

STOP YOUR WHINING!

How we must grieve the heart of God when we only complain about the very things' He blesses us with!

Besides, why would God want to bless you with more if you are not thankful for what you already have?

We gripe at our kids for wanting the bigger, better toys and instead, tell them to be thankful for what they have. Yet, we do not even do that ourselves! Maybe the kids are following the example they see at home?

*"Keep your life free from the love of money,
and be content with what you have, for He has
said, "I will never leave you nor forsake you."*

Hebrews 13:5

Stop whining about what everybody else has and, instead, be content with what God has blessed you with.

Be thankful for dirty dishes; it means you have something to eat.

It is All in Your Perception

There were two criminals on two crosses. In between those two crosses was a beaten and bruised Jesus.

One criminal mocked Jesus and hurled insults at Him.

*"Didn't you say you were the Messiah?! If so,
then save yourself and us!"*

Luke 23:39

On the other side of Jesus, there was someone else who had the same account of the details. He had something to say, too.

*"But the other criminal rebuked him. 'Don't you
fear God,' he said, 'since you are under the same
sentence? We are punished justly, for we are
getting what our deeds deserve. But this man has
done nothing wrong.'"*

Luke 23:40-41

Each criminal saw and heard the same exact thing during the crucifixion; yet, each had a completely opposite perspective and response to the situation.

One used sarcasm and implied that Jesus was not who He said He was, and one believed Him.

The criminal, who believed Jesus, said:

> *"Jesus, remember me when you come into your kingdom."*
>
> *"Jesus answered him, "Truly I tell you, today you will be with me in paradise."*
>
> *Luke 23:42-43*

The response of each in their current circumstance was ultimately a determining factor in their future destination.

Sometimes, our situations may seem difficult, but how you handle it has a big impact in the end result.

Encouragement for Your Life

We simply waste too much time on things that truly do not matter and often neglect the most precious things.

We spend more time with social media than our families, more time playing video games than talking to our kids, spend more time texting with others when you have someone special sitting right next to you, and treat those closest to us worse than we treat everybody else.

My friends, this has to stop! Our priorities are out of whack!

Are those things wrong? Of course not. But when they dominate you which, in turn, takes you away from the gifts God has given you, then that is when they become "wrong."

Cherish that husband/wife you have; the one you committed your life to. Spend time investing in those kids of yours who view you as their hero even though they just drew a picture on your wall with a marker.

Have game nights, walks in the park, sit at the dinner table together without the cell phones, etc.

Yes, take time for yourself to refuel and recharge. Just do not let that get in the way and cause you to miss out on the best blessings' life has to offer!

> *"Do nothing out of selfish ambition or vain conceit. Rather, in humility value others above yourselves."*
>
> *Philippians 2:3*
>
> *"However, each one of you also must love his wife as he loves himself, and the wife must respect her husband."*
>
> *Ephesians 5:33*

The word "love" here is the Greek word, "agape" that we will examine a little further in the next chapter. This love is not about the emotional butterflies you get because you are "in love." This is an unconditional love that you do by choice with no expectations of getting something in return. It is the highest form of love in existence.

Therefore, choose to love your spouse, honor them, respect them, do not take them for granted, and you may have heard this before: cherish them! The time to do that is now and not the funeral home!

I encourage you to kiss and hug your spouse before you depart for the day, and if you have kids, do it in front of them! They will survive it, even if they say, "Ewww! That's gross!" You are setting an example to not take life for granted!

Then, be gross again when you get home!

Do you know what you are showing them? That it is perfectly fine to love your spouse because, unfortunately, the world's definition of love is changing and becoming void of substance. They will be blessed because of it!

However, if your marriage is struggling, God is the God of restoration, and He wants to do exactly that for you. Your marriage is worth the effort, so find someone to talk to and allow God to work His restoration miracles in your life!

STOP YOUR WHINING about all you think is wrong and find those things that are precious and cling to them. You will not regret it, I promise!

Family is such a beautiful entity and we need to be treating it as such. Treasure your every moment and hold dearly to the most precious gift God has given us on this earth!

Stop Your Whining!

"Do everything without grumbling or arguing..."

Philippians 2:14

Ah oh!

Whether you are a Christian or not, we all know the story of the Israelites wandering around in the wilderness for 40 years. Did you know the trip was only supposed to take 11 days? You read that correctly; 11 days!

Unfortunately for the Israelites, they had a whining problem over just about everything.

They grumbled against their leader, they grumbled against God, they grumbled about where they used to be versus their current status, etc. causing them to miss the blessings God was putting right before them!

Because of this attitude, the trip that was supposed to be an 11-day journey turned into 40 years. At that, only three of the Israelites over 20 years old even made it to the promised land.

Are you wandering around in the wilderness today? Does everything that happens cause you to whine and complain? Do you whine about things that really are blessings?

It is time for an attitude check and if needed, some attitude adjustments!

STOP YOUR WHINING, SERIOUSLY!

CHAPTER 11: Eternal Security

It seems like I have heard that how you respond to situations is a major factor in your future destination.

Like the criminals on either side of Jesus who made their decisions, you have to make one as well.

These two criminals were guilty. They both also had a chance to be acquitted.

When the one criminal believed Jesus in who He said He was, Jesus immediately acquitted him of all sin and that criminal was made righteous in God's sight. That one decision gave him the gift of eternal security. Note that the criminal did absolutely nothing to "earn it, but simply confessed that Jesus was Lord.

We stand in the same position as these two criminals. We can either believe Jesus for who He said He was, or we can reject that message, hurl insults at Him, and then mock Him.

Your Destination Depends on Your Decision

"That at the name of Jesus every knee should bow in Heaven and on earth and under the earth, and every tongue acknowledge that Jesus Christ is Lord, to the glory of God the Father."

Philippians 2:10-11

Every "being" will do this. We can freely choose to do this right now, and it is an awesome thing! Or, we can deny the Truth and still have to do it when we get to eternity.

I believe you are intelligent enough to realize that each of these choices result in two separate destinations. I promise you; there is no comparison as to which is the better option!

This is why this chapter is included. I want you to know the same Christ who has walked with me is the same Christ who wants to walk with you, especially if you do not know Him.

If you do know Him, then my encouragement for you is to get to know Him on a deeper level.

If you do not know Him, I want to present Him to you! He is beautiful!

This is a major factor in why I have been able to move on. I know that Sherry is in paradise, which again, was solidly confirmed in the vision and confirmation by my friend. She is certainly dancing in her peach-colored dress!

> *"He will wipe away every tear from their eyes, and death shall be no more, neither shall there be mourning, nor crying, nor pain anymore, for the former things have passed away."*
>
> *Revelation 21:4*

That is a pretty good deal!

What a beautiful hope we have for those of us who know Jesus!

Do you know what else is a good deal? How about somebody paying off your debt so you do not have to? Check this out....

Debt Free!

Once we accept Jesus, He forgives our debt (sin). Why is this significant?

Someone has to pay the debt for our sin and there are only two choices:

- You can pay it or
- Jesus can pay it.

> *"For the wages of sin is (spiritual) death, but the (free) gift of God is eternal life through Christ Jesus our Lord."*
>
> *Romans 6:23*

The cool thing is that the debt has already been paid. It is as simple as accepting the best gift ever!

Your Questions Answered

"Yeah, but I already believe in God."

> *"You believe that there is one God. Good! Even the demons believe that... and shutter!"*
>
> *James 2:19*

"But you have no idea what I have done. I have done so much wrong. No way God would forgive me. I am just too messed up."

WRONG

> *"If we confess our sins, He is faithful and just to forgive us our sins and cleanse us from all unrighteousness."*
>
> *1 John 1:9*

"But I believe if you are a good person, you will make it."

> *"And if by grace, then salvation cannot be based on works; if it were, grace would no longer be grace."*
>
> *Romans 11:6*

"I will come to Jesus once I get my life together and cleaned up."

> *"….. I tell you, today is the day of God's favor, now is the day of salvation."*
>
> *2 Corinthians 6:2*

"So, let me get this straight: although I have been in sin all these years, Christ still died for me knowing what I have done?"

Yes!

"And if I accept this free gift of salvation, I get to go to Heaven?"

Yes!

"And that means I do not have to pay for my sins in hell?"

Yes!

"All I have to do is accept Jesus as my Savior?"

BINGO!

"And then God will help clean me up and lead me on the right path as I develop a relationship with Him?"

You better believe it!

Agape Love

Agape love is the type of love God gives. It is a purposeful decision to love, not based on the quality of the person being loved but is based on the character of the person doing the loving.

In other words, we cannot earn this type of love.

It finds worth in the worthless; hope in the helpless, beauty in the unlikeable, love in the unlovable, well, I think you get the point.

Here is a great example of this type of love:

"But God demonstrates His own (agape) love for us in this: while we were still sinners, , Christ died for us."

Romans 5:8

This is why we do not have to "get cleaned up first" before coming to Him. He paid for our sins while we were still a mess; therefore, we can come to Him…. while we are still a mess!

PAUL: A Great Example of Agape Love Extended

Paul was a man who wrote approximately 30% of the new testament. Before he had the infamous encounter with Christ on the road to Damascus (read it for yourself in Acts 9) , do you know what he was doing? He was <u>murdering</u> Christians!

Check out how Paul describes himself in one of his writings:

"Even though I was once a blasphemer and a persecutor and a violent man, I was shown mercy because I acted in ignorance and unbelief."

1 Timothy 1:13

If God can call a murderer to write a significant amount of the new testament, much of it about love and how to live, and be shown mercy as Paul describes in these verses:

"The grace of our Lord was poured out on me abundantly, along with the faith and love that are in Christ Jesus.

Here is a trustworthy saying that deserves full acceptance: Christ Jesus came into the world to save sinners—of whom I am the worst.

But for that very reason I was shown mercy so that in me, the worst of sinners, Christ Jesus might display his immense patience as an example for those who would believe in him and receive eternal life."

1 Timothy 1:14-16

If He can do this for Paul, "the worst of sinners," why would He not be able to call you to salvation as well?

His love for us is so much deeper than we can comprehend! This is why He, well, paid off your debt if you just accept the gift!

So, do you know Him? Would you like someone else to pay off your debt for your sin?

How Do I Become a Christian?

This is a simple concept that has an abundance of information within each concept. We will stick with the basics:

- Believe who Jesus says He is (like the criminal!) and that God raised Him from the dead.
- Confess your sins to Him to have them forgiven so your debt is paid in full.
- Ask Him to enter your heart and confess Him as Lord and Savior of your life.

Do you want to know this Jesus? Are you on a prodigal's journey and ready to return home? Then, let's go!

If you want to be debt free and are ready to become a follower of Christ, you can say this simple prayer with sincerity:

> *"Dear Jesus, I believe in you. I believe you came and died for my sins and that God raised you from the dead. I lay down my sins at your feet and ask you to forgive me for the sins I have committed. I ask for you to come into my heart, make me a new creature according to 2 Corinthians 5:17. I confess you as my Lord and Savior, and I give my life to you. I will grasp on to you and follow you from this day forward. In Jesus' name I pray, AMEN!"*

If you meant that and prayed that for the first time, then welcome to the family!

In the next chapter, there will be several Bible verses to get you started on this new journey to help you start putting that foundation on The Rock!

If you just rededicated, then welcome BACK to the family!

I strongly encourage you to read your Bible every single day. That is how your faith will grow.

> *"Faith comes by hearing, and hearing by the Word of God."*
>
> *Romans 10:17*

God is all about having a relationship with you, so also make sure to have a daily prayer life. This can be in the morning when you wake up, while you are taking a shower, on your drive to work, etc. Just make sure you are communicating with Him daily!

Then, find yourself an uncompromising, Bible-believing church to help you grow and continue to build your relationship and knowledge of Him.

Feel free to visit my official website and drop me a message to let me know of this new beginning in your life!

You can also submit any questions or comments there as well!

For the rest of you, I have one more thing to say:

Be thankful for what God has blessed you with, and....

STOP YOUR WHINING!

CHAPTER 12: Scriptures

H ere are some verses for you to get started on or continue your journey. The version used here is the Amplified version to help you understand better.

The words in brackets are not found in the verse itself. They are there to elaborate and expand on what is being said.

2 Corinthians 5:17

Therefore if anyone is in Christ [that is, grafted in, joined to Him by faith in Him as Savior], he is a new creature [reborn and renewed by the Holy Spirit]; the old things [the previous moral and spiritual condition] have passed away. Behold, new things have come [because spiritual awakening brings a new life].

As a bonus for you, I want to dig down into this verse.

I have learned that reading the Bible is more than just "reading the surface."

The new testament was written in Greek, so, I am replacing the English words in this verse with the definitions of the Greek words. The way it came out was astonishing! Here it is for your enjoyment! Check out the power behind this verse when you become a Christian!

"Therefore, if anyone is in Christ, he is new in quality, fresh in development, fresh in opportunity, because he has not been found like this before.

He is a new creature which has been founded from nothing.

The ancient and longstanding things have been rendered void and disregarded. Behold, fresh and unused things have come into being."

How awesome is that?!

-

Romans 8:24

"Being justified [declared free of the guilt of sin, made acceptable to God, and granted eternal life] as a gift by His [precious, undeserved] grace, through the redemption [the payment for our sin] which is [provided] in Christ Jesus."

-

Titus 3:4-7

(4) "But when the goodness and kindness of God our Savior and His love for mankind appeared [in human form as the Man, Jesus Christ],

(5) He saved us, not because of any works of righteousness that we have done, but because of His own compassion and mercy, by the cleansing of the new birth (spiritual transformation, regeneration) and renewing by the Holy Spirit,

(6) whom He poured out richly upon us through Jesus Christ our Savior,

(7) so that we would be justified [made free of the guilt of sin] by His [compassionate, undeserved] grace, and that we would be [acknowledged as acceptable to Him and] made heirs of eternal life [actually experiencing it] according to our hope (His guarantee)."

-

Isaiah 43:18-19

(18) "Do not remember the former things, Or ponder the things of the past."

(19) Listen carefully, I am about to do a new thing, now it will spring forth; Will you not be aware of it? I will even put a road in the wilderness, Rivers in the desert."

Philippians 1:6

"I am convinced and confident of this very thing, that He who has begun a good work in you will [continue to] perfect and complete it until the day of Christ Jesus [the time of His return]."

-

Jeremiah 29:11

*"For I know the plans and thoughts that I have for you,' says the L*ORD*, 'plans for peace and well-being and not for disaster, to give you a future and a hope."*

-

Deuteronomy 31:6

*"Be strong and courageous, do not be afraid or tremble in dread before them, for it is the L*ORD *your God who goes with you. He will not fail you or abandon you."*

-

Jeremiah 17:7

*"Blessed [with spiritual security] is the man who believes and trusts in and relies on the L*ORD *And whose hope and confident expectation is the L*ORD*."*

HEBREWS 10:17

"AND THEIR SINS AND THEIR LAWLESS ACTS I WILL REMEMBER NO MORE *[no longer holding their sins against them]."*

-

Ephesians 2:8

"For it is by grace [God's remarkable compassion and favor drawing you to Christ] that you have been saved [actually delivered from judgment and given eternal life] through faith. And this [salvation] is not of yourselves [not through your own effort], but it is the [undeserved, gracious] gift of God;"

-

2 Corinthians 5:21

"He made Christ who knew no sin to [judicially] be sin on our behalf, so that in Him we would become the righteousness of God [that is, we would be made acceptable to Him and placed in a right relationship with Him by His gracious lovingkindness]."

Romans 8:1

"Therefore there is now no condemnation [no guilty verdict, no punishment] for those who are in Christ Jesus [who believe in Him as personal Lord and Savior]."

To reiterate:

Make sure to stay in the Word daily!

You have a spirit man (literally) that needs to be fed. Feeding your physical body only once or twice per week will cause it to be sick and malnourished. Your spirit man works the same way as the physical body. So, make sure the spirit is fed plenty with the Word!

And again, develop a prayer life and find a Bible believing church to help your relationship with Christ grow!

For the seasoned Christians, I challenge you to step it up!

Blessings to each and every one of you, and may God's strength, peace, and favor rest on you as you get to know Him in a deeper, more personal way.

God Bless!

Epilogue

I was going to write an epilogue, but God blessed me with a beautiful, new bride, so the epilogue is still being written…

Contact Information

If you would like to book John to speak, you can use the contact information below.

He can speak at your church, men's conference, marriage conference, etc.

You may also send him any comments or questions you may have using the contact form on the official website.

John Helton Speaking Ministries

There you will find information about:

- **Speaking Ministry**
- **Marriage and Couples Ministry**
- **Relationship, Bereavement, & Professional Coaching**
- **And watch the Legally Blind Guy:**
  - **Bowl**
  - **Play Drums**
  - **Organize a Concert**

Phone: (502) 219-7590

Website: TheBlindFury.com, MaritalMonkey.com, TheBloodWall.com

For Booking: Booking@TheBlindFury.com

Made in the USA
Monee, IL
17 June 2020